CW00498532

12-Week Couples Therapy Workbook

Essential Exercises for Enhancing Communication Skills, Deepening Intimacy, and Strengthening Your Relationship through Emotionally Focused Therapy (EFT)

Published by: Stanley Sheppard

Complimentary Worksheets and more

Elevate your relationship to new heights! Unlock three powerful bonuses – a dynamic relationship worksheet, engaging conversation cards, and a comprehensive couple's planner.

To get access go to webpage or scan a QR code:

https://greatlifebooks.com/Couples

- Bring new life to your relationship with our dynamic relationship worksheet.

- Explore our engaging conversation cards for some real talk that sparks meaningful conversations.

- And, don't miss out on our comprehensive couple's planner – it's not just about organizing your days but also about building and achieving dreams together.

Every day becomes a chance to strengthen the unique bond you share.

Table of Contents

Introduction

About me

Let me begin this book with something you might not be expecting: a confession.

You see, I never saw myself as the kind of man who goes to therapy. To me, sitting in a room and blurting out your deepest darkest feelings to a stranger always seemed pretty much like torture. In my world, therapy was something women did, and men too, rarely, if the women around them pushed hard enough. In fact, this is my confession: I initially only went to therapy because my wife threatened to leave unless I did.

Let me tell the story from the beginning. What I want you to understand is that my wife and I didn't just love each other – we *adored* one another. I used to joke that my life could be broken neatly into two parts, BK and AK, Before Katie and After Katie. I can't remember what life was like before I knew she existed, but I will tell you that the day I met her, it was as though everything exploded into rich, three-dimensional technicolor for the first time. Nothing was ever the same again.

How can I summarize a love, a lifetime? We lived in a little two bedroom with a great garden, we had a pair of cats, and a string of mostly happy Christmases and Valentine's Days. Katie was a lecturer at the local art college, and I plugged away at a boring but stable IT job. We played other roles, too. She was girlfriend, and wife, and eventually mother. On bad days she was *The Nag* and *The Eternally Disappointed One*. On good days she was *My Rock* and *The Only Good Thing That Has Ever Happened to Me.*

My roles changed over time, too. I played reluctant boyfriend, then boyfriend, then ex-boyfriend, then boyfriend again, then husband, then father. I'll admit that for a while in the beginning, I starred exclusively as *Bad Father*. On good days my wife cast me as *My Hero* and even *My Everything*. We went through periods, though, where I was *Annoying Roommate* and (I shudder) *Mr. Man Child*.

You get the idea. Our relationship was real, and it was messy, and it was human. Older and wiser now, I think that this is what all relationships are like, in their own special ways. If you've picked up this book, I suspect that *your* relationship, though it's nothing like mine, has just the same messiness, and realness, and humanness.

You're probably wondering when I tell you the part of the story where the wheels came off. Well, though it happened a full nine years into our marriage, I almost think that our problems started much earlier – that is, on the day we met. We had been struggling for a long time when Katie finally sat me down one day and told me that unless I went to therapy with her, we were over. In hindsight, it was the kindest, bravest thing she could have done. In that moment, however, it felt like being held hostage at gunpoint. I agreed, desperate, and off we went.

Ladies and gentlemen, couple's therapy did *not* fix our relationship.

What it did was leave me confused, hurt, hundreds of dollars poorer, and with a lifelong hatred for the phrase, "let's unpack that." Like many people seeking mental health care, I'm sorry to say that the experience was extremely hit and miss – with more miss than hit. I felt like the therapist inevitably took my wife's "side" (yes, I admit that back then I was still thinking of "sides"). Katie felt like I was being stubborn, and that if only I'd just open up more, we'd all magically heal and live happily ever after.

We churned over the thing for a few months, but at last we had to admit the writing was on the wall. It was over. We agreed to a trial separation.

I will never forget how cold and grey the house felt that morning she left for her mother's.

Now, bear with me, because this bleak story does have a happy ending, I promise.

The day I met my wife, I fell in love with her, and it only took a moment. A split second. No time at all. But learning how to kindle that precious spark and take care of it, day after day, and nurture it into a strong, warming fire was something that took me *years*. It's something that I'm still not done learning. Falling in love with my wife for the first time was the easiest thing in the world. Knowing how to *keep* falling in love with her, every day, every moment after that… now that was a learning curve.

To cut a (very) long story short, we both cooled off and, in a few months, we tentatively decided to try just one more time. We attempted therapy. Again. But this time, we did things differently. We signed up for an "EFT couple's course," dove head-first into the workbooks and spent many, many evenings having difficult but fruitful conversations. Some of what we tried worked, and some of it didn't. But gradually, we clawed our way back to one another, and the path we took to get there inspired the book you are now holding in your hands.

Today, I'm not the man I was when I first met my wife. Nether, for that matter, is Katie the same woman. One of the paradoxes of human relationships is that we often need to transform dramatically in order to most fully be ourselves. I've learnt that **human beings are relational to their very core** – we are not just in relationship with one another, we *are* these relationships. The way we connect and communicate defines who we are. From a man who used to think that emotional expression was best relegated to cheesy daytime TV drama, this was a transformation indeed!

I am more in love with my wife today than ever before. I believe the real romance begins long after the meet cute, long after love-at-first-sight. It may seem strange to say, but real romance is picking up a book on couple's therapy because deep down, you are willing to do the work, and to fight for what really matters. For what you love. That's what this book is ultimately about: love.

In the chapters that follow, I'll be sharing the insights, methods, techniques, theories and approaches that helped me rescue my own relationship from the brink. My wife and I blundered through our own journey with plenty of trial and error, but so much of the hard stuff could have been avoided. You're about to read the material I wished we both had nine years ago.

About this book

I wrote this book for all those struggling couples who want desperately to find a way to work things out, but just don't know where to start. If it can help just one couple find more compassion and joy with one another, then I'll know that my own tribulations with my wife were worth it.

No matter your age, background, orientation or identity, if your relationship is "on the rocks" then this book is for you. In the pages that follow I'll talk about a particular kind of relationship (straight, married, kids… you know the drill) but the insights I want to share here go far beyond these details. Underneath all the infinite uniqueness and variation in the relationships we human beings form, I believe at root that all of us are seeking our own vision of connectedness, understanding, empathy and belonging. We thrive on it. We're built for it.

I'm going to be real with you, though: the work covered in this book is just that. Work. A big reason that therapy failed the first time for Katie and I was that we simply didn't commit to it. Sure, we talked (good lord, did we talk!) but we were relatively low on action. That's why this book will contain plenty of practical exercises to try out, so you can apply each concept and make it come to life for you, in your unique situation.

The book outlines a comprehensive twelve-week program carefully designed to accompany you on a well-worn path to a stronger, happier and healthier connection to your partner. Some of the ideas will seem familiar to you, others less so. I guarantee that all of them, however, will take on extra dimension and meaning when you consciously lift them off these pages and bring them into your living, breathing relationship.

I know it's tempting to simply read through everything in one go, but I strongly encourage you to slow down and take the full twelve weeks to give yourself and your partner time to digest the material. Be patient. Unlike other books, even other self-help books, this is one that's been written with the express intention of being *shared*. It's a collaboration. Every week's module will contain the same ingredients:

1. I'll share a **key concept** or idea to reflect on during the week.

2. We'll look at **real-life couples** of all kinds who are experiencing issues in this area.

3. Then you'll try out a **practical exercise** as a couple, to apply the key concept.

Through the guided exercises and tools, you get to develop the key concept in your own relationship. The real-life couples are there to show you what that may look like in a hypothetical relationship, but don't get too hung up on these – every relationship is unique, and some of these couples will feel more relatable to you than others.

Try to dedicate an hour or two once a week to working through each module. You might choose to read through each section on your own, then meet up with your partner to attempt the exercises as a team. You might take an extra week or two if the module proves especially relevant. And of course, I heartily encourage you to experiment with the exercises to make them your own.

How you do the program is adaptable, but what's non-negotiable is that you bring a genuine sense of commitment and curiosity to the process. In relationships, you get out what you put in, and it's the same here. You won't experience the full benefit of the process if you attempt it half-heartedly, or if only one half of the couple steers, while the other half is merely a passenger.

That leads me to a necessary caveat before we continue: this book is not for everyone. I'm the world's biggest believer in people's ability to transform, and create the loving, healthy relationships of their dreams. I have that faith because I have experienced that transformation myself. That said, please do not attempt this program if you are in a relationship where there is abuse of any kind. Therapy, including self-directed workbooks like this one, is not appropriate in abusive dynamics, and can make things worse. If you're experiencing physical, emotional, sexual or financial abuse, I implore you to seek more appropriate help elsewhere.

That said, a relationship doesn't have to be abusive to make it ineligible for EFT interventions. This book was written for couples where **both** parties are at least willing to explore the issue and commit to the exercises. I say "at least willing" because I get it – when a relationship is in crisis mode, there can be a serious shortage of kind feelings, and a loss of trust can make people hesitant to put in the work.

I want to assure you that feeling this way is perfectly normal and expected. A relationship in crisis is by definition one where communication has broken down, and introducing a workbook like this can feel awkward, vulnerable and even a little scary. But committing to the program doesn't mean making any serious promises, closing any doors, or forcing any conclusions.

All you are committing to is an open mind.

If both people are ready to genuinely try something new, then that's a solid start. I can guarantee you – beautiful things can grow from that tiny seed.

About EFT

The theoretical approach we'll be using in this book is called Emotion-focused therapy, or EFT for short. It was developed by Sue Johnson and Leslie Greenberg in 1985 and, after decades of empirical validation, the approach is still popular today. In 1988 the pair published a couple's therapy manual (*Emotionally Focused Therapy for Couples*) and much of the material you're about to read has been inspired by the principles first introduced in its pages.

The key is in the name: this approach puts emotions front and center, because it understands emotion as core to human being's identity, relationships… and relationship problem. Simply, if we are lacking in emotional awareness or ability to regulate our own feelings, we're liable to encounter problems in our lives, whether that's with decision-making, finding purpose and meaning, or being resilient in the face of everyday adversity.

Because EFT is so focused on improving your understanding of your own emotions, and how they relate to your thoughts and behavior, it plays a special role in couples' counselling. The idea is that by taking ownership of your own emotional patterns, as well as the patterns of your partner, you understand how you're mutually creating larger, overarching patterns together, as a pair.

With a special blend of awareness, acceptance and the courage to make gentle changes, EFT can help both individuals and couples become more "emotionally literate."

As you may have gathered, I used to harbor a deep mistrust of "feeling talk" because I saw it as passive, unnecessary and, if I'm honest, a little indulgent. I have always valued *action*, and so dwelling on emotion seemed pointless at best and a distraction at worst. This is where people can misunderstand the purpose of emotions, and the purpose of emotion-focused work: we do not process feelings *instead* of taking action. We process our feelings *so that* we can take action.

Only once an individual becomes aware of what they're feeling, can they accept that reality with compassion, and start to transform those emotions in concrete ways, according to their own values and goals. Awareness of emotions is always the first step.

Personally, I always shied away from exploring emotions because, well, I was afraid. The irony is that by refusing to face my emotions and proactively work with them, I was actually ensuring I'd never give myself the opportunity to release them fully and move on.

Using EFT, Katie and I learnt to:

- Be aware of what we're feeling (this was tough for me)

- Welcome that feeling, whatever it is, without judgment (this was really tough for Katie)

- Describe our experience in words

- Evaluate whether emotions were useful or not

- Manage, regulate and moderate those emotions

- And finally, communicate all the above to one another, with compassion and clarity (I'm not going to lie, we're both still working on this one!).

If this seems like an intimidating list, you're not alone. When Katie and I started our journey together, we were exploring uncharted territory, both as individuals and together. It was daunting. The big Eureka moment came when I understood that **emotions are valuable**. They serve a purpose, and the better you become at mastering, accepting and using them, the more robust your mental health will be, and the more your relationships will flourish. That's what EFT is all about.

For this kind of therapy to work its magic, a certain level of honesty is required, as well as a mega-dose of compassion. You'll be taking deep dives into your attachment styles, the roles you've played in your family history, the way you've learnt to approach problems, the set of narratives and thought patterns you've carried through life, your identity and learnt behavior, your existential hangups, your traumas, your needs and all those dark corners of your psyche that feel a little scary to admit to…

To do any of this work, you're going to need to be kind and gentle with yourself. What's more, you're going to be getting up close and personal with all your partner's attachment styles, roles, history, patterns, identities, hangups, traumas, needs and dark corners. Again, to do this requires an enormous amount of respect, tenderness and care.

As we move through each week, you'll be prompted to work through an exercise, but for now, it's enough to check in with some core principles that inform the spirit of the work we'll be doing together. EFT often plays out in a series of exercises, but it's also an attitude – a *way* of approaching yourself, your partner, and the world in general. By adopting this mindset, you'll be positioning yourself to receive the best of what this process has to offer.

4 Key Principles of EFT

Emotions are dynamic and experiential

The work happens in the here and now, in the connection, in the conversation. It unfolds, moment by moment, and it's a living, breathing thing. Insights come from the raw, real back-and-forth, and from active interaction with your partner.

Think of the process not as some private, abstract thing you read in a book, but something shared and co-created with your partner. More of a live jam session than a carefully rehearsed solo piece!

Emotions require our awareness

You cannot master and understand your emotions unless you acknowledge that they're happening in the first place, and how to talk about them. Though couples' EFT is about connection, engagement and dialogue with your partner, it also requires that you periodically look within and take responsibility for recognizing your own emotional state.

Emotions need to be expressed

Most people know that communication is key in relationships, but communication of what? To reach out and connect with our partners, we need to be able to clearly express our feelings, our needs, and our limitations. If we cannot accept and understand our own emotions, we cannot expect others to, right?

Emotions can be regulated

That said, we are not defined by our emotional experience in any one moment. Another one of my big misconceptions (I admit, I've had a few!) was that feeling and accepting your emotions means being mindlessly at their mercy. Nothing could be further from the truth. EFT teaches us that from our understanding and acceptance of emotions comes the ability to regulate them. We can honor and accept our feelings *without* putting them in charge.

If all of that seems reasonable to you, and you're ready to take your first step on your EFT journey, then we'll jump right in. You and your partner will need a notebook, some regularly scheduled quiet time, a little curiosity and a whole lot of faith. Are you ready?

Week 1

Setting the Foundation

"Love takes off masks that we fear we cannot live without and know we cannot live within." ~ James Baldwin

Let's start at the beginning. When I say beginning, I really mean it – we'll begin in childhood, where all our early relational patterns were first laid down.

We all come into this world utterly dependent on others for survival, and our ability to bond and attach to the primary caregivers in our lives is literally a matter of life and death. If our caregivers are generally available and meet our needs, we attach well, and these early experiences become the template onto which we build all our future adult relationships. To the extent that our earliest needs are not met, however, we may acquire distortions to this original blueprint, and inherit a legacy of insecure attachment that remains long after we've grown up and no longer depend on our parents.

In fact, we carry those patterns, distortions and injuries with us into adulthood, where we not only play out our own learnt behaviors in relating, but we also find ourselves gravitating towards other people with relational wounds that resonate with our own. When I first met Katie, it was as though we were two puzzle pieces who had found one another… the "click" between us was palpable. I didn't know at the time that certain hidden, unconscious parts of us were clicking, too.

Finding your attachment style

When I was younger, I was the quiet guy with a motorcycle and a vow that I'd be tied down by nothing and no man – or no woman, I should say. I was ferociously independent and fond of telling the girls I dated that I didn't do "labels" and the moment they tried to weasel a commitment out of me, I'd be gone like the wind. I wouldn't be controlled.

I pitied my friends who had gotten tangled in messy arrangements with women who only wanted to limit their freedom. I liked having a girlfriend, sure, but I'd quietly check out if I felt that anyone was expecting too much of me. I was a closed book. I didn't need anyone, and I got antsy if others tried to need me.

That all changed when I met Katie, of course. Before I knew what was happening, I'd fallen head over heels. I'd never felt so vulnerable in my life. She was a gamechanger and she knew it. But Katie was also clingy and demanding and had very little sense of personal space. She'd call me multiple times every day, desperate for reassurance. She said "I love you" first and waited, big puppy eyes staring at me, until I said it too.

Years later, our therapist claimed that I was the "distancer" in the relationship, and Katie was the "pursuer." She chased me, and I ran away. The more I ran, the more anxious she got, the more she chased, the more anxious I got… and on and on. Today I understand that it all comes down to attachment styles, and ingrained behaviors that Katie and I had learnt long before we first laid eyes on one another.

What's your attachment style?

What's your partner's?

Most importantly, how are your styles *interacting*?

What follows is a description of what has been identified as the four major attachment styles. Attachment theory originally stemmed from work done in the 60s and 70s by developmental psychologist Mary Ainsworth but was later developed by John Bowlby in his complete seminal work, *Attachment and Loss* (1969–82). Both Ainsworth and Bowlby described attachment in terms of the natural and healthy human tendency to return to the "safe base" of a primary caregiver during times of distress.

The following descriptions come from clinical research done on infants and the characteristic ways they respond to their primary caregiver leaving the room and then returning. These patterns have been found to be remarkably stable and predictive of later adult relationship behavior and are found in all cultures. Read through each description and see which one resonates, and how many of the statements you agree with. Then, have your partner do the same.

Secure attachment style

Securely attached children are distressed when a caregiver leaves, but when the caregiver returns, the child can be soothed and quickly calms down. Such a child learns to emotionally regulate and overall feels safe enough to explore their environment and trust other people.

Securely attached adults are:

- Comfortable and confident in who they are as people

- Not afraid that others will abandon, reject or dislike them

- Able to give and receive love easily

- Good communicators, who are at ease expressing their needs and limits

- Able to be intimate but enjoy independence too

Insecure-anxious style

These children are distressed when the caregiver leaves, but curiously are not soothed or calmed when the caregiver returns. It's as though they have lost their trust in the caregiver and feel anxious that they are not fundamentally taken care of, even when the caregiver is present. This rupture in a sense of security in the world may manifest as feelings of resentment at the caregiver's attempts to soothe. It's as though the child believes, "you're here, but you might leave at any moment."

Insecurely attached, anxious adults are:

- So prone to craving intimacy that they rush into relationships and depend heavily on their partners to feel safe and whole

- Extremely sensitive to signs of rejection, and prone to jealousy or hypervigilance

- Often unconfident and blame themselves for relationship problems

- Doubtful and clingy, sometimes falling into people-pleasing behavior

- Preoccupied with doing whatever it takes to avoid being abandoned, and constantly push for more closeness

Insecure-avoidant style

Some children respond to the absence of their caregiver by a seeming lack of interest. When heart rates and blood pressure are measured, these children *are* extremely distressed, but they do not express it. Instead, they feign indifference. It's as though they have determined that the caregiver is not responsive to their needs and have quietly given up attempts to win it back or express their distress.

Insecurely attached, avoidant adults are:

- Extremely independent and self-sufficient, unable to trust others easily

- Uncomfortable with intimacy, vulnerability and emotional closeness, finding it suffocating or even a threat

- More likely to end a relationship that's going well, or passively withdraw and escape

- Often described as "blowing hot and cold" and tend to feel smothered when people get too close or make what feel like unreasonable emotional demands

- Uncomfortable committing, and tend to place their own needs before their partner's

Fearful-avoidant style

The least common attachment style is sometimes called *chaotic* or *disorganized*. This happens when the caregiver is perceived by the child to be frightening or in some way a danger. The dilemma for such a child is that the person who they rely on for survival is also a person who simultaneously threatens that survival.

Understandably, this damages the child's sense of security not just with their caregiver, but with all people, and the world at large. Adults who have been abused or neglected as children may crave intimacy and yet respond to it erratically. These are the children who have no fixed pattern of response to a returning caregiver – they seem lost and volatile, unable to settle.

Fearfully avoidant adults are:

- A confusing mix of anxious and avoidant behaviors

- Often plagued by mixed feelings about other people

- Liable to have irregular, dramatic or generally disorganized relationships with others

- Unable to relax with trustworthy partners, but also unable to recognize partners who are genuinely unhealthy for them, or even dangerous

If you guessed that I have an insecure-avoidant type, and that Katie has an insecure-anxious type, then you guessed right. In fact, this pairing is a fairly common one.

Now, you may occasionally see the above types given slightly different names, and some researchers have expanded or collapsed certain categories, but the general principle remains. By understanding your own attachment style, you understand the relational blueprint that was created early in childhood, and how this influences everything from the way you communicate, to your problem-solving style and how you face conflict in relationships.

Depending on your own ingrained patterns, you may find yourself in relationships with other people that reinforce that early dynamic, so you play out the old psychodrama again and again. In this way, relationships become echoes of our earliest experiences.

A common example is a woman with an insecure-anxious style who repeatedly finds herself embroiled with emotionally unavailable men who keep abandoning her, no matter how much she begs and pleads. Or consider the insecure-avoidant man who shuns emotional intimacy but is secretly desperate for it. He may find himself forever claiming he is "not looking for anything serious" … and yet he's always getting trapped in relationships that are extremely serious!

The ideal, of course, is two securely attached people in a healthy, fulfilling relationship with one another. They grow in trust and intimacy, communicating openly and respectfully, consciously enjoying their intimacy together.

Week 1 Exercise

Step 1

Begin by identifying your own attachment style and invite your partner to do the same. It's possible for there to be some overlap, but chances are you fall predominantly into one or other broad category.

If you're stumped, a fascinating thing to do is ask your partner which one they'd choose for you, based on what they know about you. Because these attachment categories are about patterns of relating, your partner may have a unique insight into your tendencies and communication styles. Do they find that you seek to escape intimacy or that you're always pushing for more? Are you trusting in other people or are you more doubtful of securing the love you need?

Step 2

Once you both have an idea of the ingrained attachment patterns you both inherited from childhood, use the following questions to start a conversation about how these attachment styles may be playing out now, in the present:

How does your attachment style influence the way you communicate?

How do you respond to your partner's bids for affection and intimacy?

If your two attachment styles were having a conversation together, what would that conversation be like?

Step 3

After you've gained a better understanding of how you and your partner's attachment styles are interacting, you can start to explore how this may be feeding into the current issues facing your relationship. For now, attempt this part of the exercise *individually*. In the coming week, separately spend some time assessing the current state of your relationship, and reflecting on where you are now, both as individuals and as a couple. With compassion and curiosity, write a few notes identifying two things:

1. Your relationship's strengths, from your perspective

2. The areas in your relationship that you most believe need attention and development

As you write, remember that you are reflecting on the connection between you both, and not laying blame, airing grievances or making accusations. Next week, we will use these notes to guide the creation of shared relationship goals.

Nick and Violet

When Nick and Violet did the above exercise, they were surprised to see an hour-long conversation grow to three hours. Violet easily identified herself as securely attached, but Nick recognized himself in the fearful-avoidant description and attributed this to his abusive father. After much discussion, Violet could better understand that Nick's early experiences meant he sometimes perceived her ordinary request to communicate as emotionally loaded and even manipulative.

The two realized that a big part of their relationship trouble came from the completely different ways they understood "communication." For Nick, the phrase "we need to talk" was secret code for "warning, you're in big trouble" whereas for Violet, wanting to communicate was normal and enjoyable, and proof that two people cared about one another. Realizing this misunderstanding, Nick and Violet knew they had work to do!

Week 2

Your Relationship Goals

"Love does not consist of gazing at each other, but in looking together in the same direction." ~ Antoine de Saint-Exupéry

When Katie and I were organizing our wedding, I was stunned at just how much planning was needed. Flowers, cake, invitations, seating, endless outfits and their endless accessories – Katie happily took care of most of it. But I do remember wondering to myself just exactly how it was that she knew to do all these things. Where was it all coming from?

It was as though Katie was receiving a signal from some mothership somewhere, beaming down instructions directly into her brain, which she dutifully carried out. She was like a salmon heading to some ancestral spawning ground, on instinct alone. She just *knew* for example, that we'd need "wedding favors." I'll be honest, I'd never heard of the things. Yet suddenly, it became absolutely essential that we pick just the right ones, buy them, and get them ready for the big day.

My point here is not about weddings. Rather, the moment was one of the first glimpses I got into the fact that Katie was operating under an entirely different set of assumptions than I was. We both wanted marriage. We both wanted a big wedding. We were on the same page, right?

Maybe not. In the months that followed, I realized that these two things represented entirely different goals for each of us. It wasn't so much that we misunderstood each other. In those early days, neither of us believed there was anything to misunderstand. I asked her if she wanted to get married, she said "yes" and so we naively concluded that our life goals were more or less aligned. Spoiler alert: they really weren't.

A role is not a goal

What is a wife?

What is a husband?

For that matter, what is a girlfriend or a boyfriend or a life partner?

When hearing any of these words, you likely have a picture in your mind of what such a person *does*. However, the real kicker is – does the other person agree with this picture? Katie and I had different pictures of "wedding." Later, we would discover that we also had different pictures of "our relationship." She had a picture of who I was supposed to be, and I had a picture of who she was supposed to be.

One of the first lessons we had to learn was that *a role is not a goal*. A relationship doesn't automatically come with its own built-in purpose and direction. It's like a car. It can be a great car and you can both be pretty happy to be driving in it together, but at some point, you have to be clear on where the car is going.

What are your relationship goals, and how do they fit with your partner's?

"I just want us to be happy." Well, that's a goal in the same way as it's a goal to say, "I just want a nice car." It doesn't tell you where the car is going, why it's going there, or what route to take. It's guaranteed that halfway along the journey you will both discover that you have different towns in mind, both of which are called "Happy", but which sadly happen to be 500 miles apart.

"I want to be a good partner, and for him to be a good partner, too." This is also not much of a goal because, well, good for what? Good in what way? To extend my metaphor even further, a caravan doing a long-distance journey to a sleepy coastal town is a "good" car, and so is a Formula One Ferrari with a single expert driver whizzing round the same track again and again. They're both *good*. Yet they are both moving towards very different goals.

This week, we're going beyond the assumptions, and looking a little deeper into what we actually want for ourselves, our lives and our relationships. Then we'll do the work of putting all our expectations, needs, assumptions, desires and goals alongside those of our partner, and seeing what that implies for our journey onward.

Last week, we spent some time exploring our relational patterns in the form of learnt attachment styles. That was the past, but what about the future? This week we consider where we want to go from here.

Individual goal setting

Let's start with you.

Most of us find the task of goal-setting more or less a boring homework exercise, as though it were too simple and obvious a thing to spend much time on. The funny thing is, when you ask people what their precise goals are, they almost never can tell you. In the place where their goals would be, there is simply a set of foregone conclusions, assumptions and possibly unrealistic expectations.

It was amusing when I discovered the existence of "wedding favors" and just how much they mattered to my wife, but it's less amusing when you consider that many of us are unaware of our partner's deeper, more unconscious expectations. I'll give you a more serious example. Katie and I happily set up a joint account to pay for share household expenses after we were married. For the most part she was in charge of keeping our financial records in check, and I was surprised to see her one day picking apart the receipt for the grocery shop we'd just done. She carefully extracted some items she said were mine alone – a bottle of whiskey, a brand of soap I liked – and asked me to settle this from my own account.

I was taken aback. She was confused, too. "People pay for their own things out of their own account" she told me. "That's obvious."

Here's the truth: none of it is "obvious." We had never formally set out the rules of how we'd split finances; we just made assumptions. My (unspoken) goal was that we'd pretty much share it all, and her things and my things would even out in the long run. Her (unspoken) goal was that to keep things fair, we'd share the absolute basics, and take care of our separate things.

The solution was clear: we needed to speak all those unspoken goals.

Before you can start comparing and contrasting your set of expectations with your partner's, however, you need to have some understanding of your own needs and desires. Easier said than done. Before embarking on the exercise that follows, spend some time contemplating the following questions on your own. Some will seem, to use Katie's word, "obvious" but answer them anyway. Sometimes, our most ingrained assumptions are actually the ones we most need to become aware of having at all.

What are your core values and guiding principles in life? These are the things that matter to you more than anything else (in the area of love and relationships, that is), and they're the things that you are unwilling to ever compromise on.

Example: "More than anything I value honesty. I need the truth and to feel like I can always trust those around me. I cannot be in a relationship where there is a shred of doubt or deception."

What are your less important preferences and inclinations? These are "nice to have" things rather than "must have" things.

Example: "I'm Brazilian and I would love to meet someone with the same background. But it's not 100% essential – it just would be nice."

Setting aside your current relationship for a moment, think carefully about what specifically you most want from a connection with another person. Don't think in abstract terms, but instead imagine what you'd concretely do, day to day, in ordinary life. What activities are you doing, for how long, when, where? Zoom in on the details.

Example: "I'm a homebody and want someone to build a nice cozy home life with. I want someone to mooch around the markets on Sunday mornings with, and be laid-back, and do DIY projects sometimes. I want to spend most days together."

Think about your "timeline." Is there a fixed relationship milestone you're aiming for? How important is this to you? Why does it matter and how much are you willing to negotiate on this? Connected to this are the big non-negotiable questions: is marriage important? Are kids important?

Example: "I don't want kids, not now, not ever. I want to be married or at least in a stable relationship, though, and I'd like to get there in the next five years or so. Marriage isn't a big deal, but monogamy sure is."

Thinking now about the things you'd like from an ideal relationship, how realistic do you think they are? Do you need to "lower your standards" … or could you stand being a little more discerning?

Example: "My ideal woman will want to be a stay-at-home mom, but I also want her to support me financially."

What sacrifices are you willing to make? I know this may seem like a hard one, but we all make compromises – which compromises would you choose? Why?

Example: "I'm willing to support a partner financially if they're unemployed, but only if they're studying to improve their career prospects."

Considering the long term, what do you anticipate needing most in five-, ten- or twenty-years' time? How might your needs change over time?

Example: "For the time being, I just want someone to have fun with and enjoy life. But I do anticipate wanting to settle down eventually, especially as I reach my late thirties."

Now, taking your answers to the above questions, loosely formulate your own relationship goals *for you as an individual*. This may be tricky but try to temporarily see yourself outside of your current situation, and just be curious about what you need, want and are aiming for. When you're feeling confident in that, have your partner do the same. Then you're ready for the next step.

Week 2 Exercise

This week we explore collaborative goal setting:

Step 1

Share. Tell your partner what your answers were, then listen without interruption as they tell you theirs. Hold off on any interpretations or judgments – just listen for now.

Step 2

Can you identify any areas of overlap in the answers you've both given? See if you can rephrase these shared values or goals as a collaborative goal for your relationship as a whole.

Step 3

Take a look at areas of potential mismatch. Again, without making it a problem, see if you can spot points of disagreement. Now, things may get interesting here, but for now just identify and explore these areas; you don't have to rush in and "fix" anything or come to any conclusions. Simply explore whether you can come to a joint understanding of what this mismatch is.

Step 4

Using what you've learnt from step 2 and 3, identify one or two goals that you can commit to as a couple for the remainder of the twelve-week program. While you might also like to privately decide on your personal goals, the key here is to agree on something *together.*

Step 5

An optional final step is to create a shared vision board to capture the essence of what you're both aiming for. You can include plenty of images and make a visual collage, or alternatively pick some quotes or symbols that best capture what you hope to achieve. Get creative!

Joel and Klara

When Joel and Klara spent some time exploring their own individual goals, they soon discovered a potential source of tension: while Klara's core values were all about adventure, learning and growth, Joel's were about safety, financial comfort and dependability. The clash became more evident as they talked. Klara saw the next five years as time for fun and travel, while Joel had simply assumed they'd soon move in together and "get more serious about our careers."

Instantly, their previous arguments made sense. While the couple could see that they had different ideas for the short term, they both discovered that they had similar visions for the longer-term future. Seeing this, they realized that they had both been rushing and putting pressure on one another. If they were headed in the same direction, could they compromise a little on the speed?

Instead of creating a vision board, they chose a special song they both felt encapsulated their new commitment to figuring things out together, and with patient kindness. They chose John Legend's Ordinary People ("cause we're ordinary people… maybe we should take it slow…") and both made promises that whatever happened in the coming twelve weeks, they would take it steady and be kind to one another.

Week 3

Effective Communication Techniques

"In the end there doesn't have to be anyone who understands you. There just has to be someone who wants to." ~ Robert Brault

You've heard it a million times before, I'm sure: communication is everything in relationships.

Without communication, there is no understanding, no trust, no intimacy. It's the first rock you lay down in the foundation of your relationship. The only way to communicate, however, is to authentically connect with our own emotional experience. Take a look at any little baby – they have no problem expressing their emotions! Yet, as we grow up, certain formative experiences (like our attachment to our caregivers we explored in the first week) can interfere with this normal and natural instinct.

If we can fully access our own feelings, then we are able to express them to the people we love – we become more real and authentic, and let me tell you, easier to love. We give the people around us a way to understand who we are and what we need. The more they can access our perspectives, fears and experiences, the more easily our partners can grab a hold of them and offer us all the compassion and understanding we crave.

When you share who you are on an emotional level, it also makes it easier for your partner to do the same. In other words, empathy is contagious! With empathy and understanding in place, conflict resolution comes much more easily. Intimacy follows. You lay down one more brick onto that foundation, and your trust in one another grows.

Sounds great, doesn't it? It doesn't always work that way, though.

The infinite argument

Here's one way it often does work.

It all begins with a trigger. For Katie and me, this trigger's name was "Valentine's Day." One day, I suddenly became aware that it was February 15th, and Katie had gone quiet. All at once a wave of negativity hit me: why was it *my* job to organize something for Valentine's Day? Why did we have to go through this ridiculous ritual when she knew very well that I loved her? How dare she get angry with me when just a few days ago, I bought her favorite ice cream, didn't I? In fact, come to think of it, she didn't say thank you at the time, did she?

With all this streaming through my mind, I decided to sulk a little myself. If she wanted to fight, well, she'd have to crack first and say something instead of being so passive aggressive, I thought.

Now, would you like to see this whole affair from Katie's point of view? It's February 10th and you start wondering if your relationship with this commitment-phobic man is ever going to amount to anything. You feel sad. All week you wonder whether you should allow yourself to hope that maybe, just maybe, he'll surprise you this year, like he promised to last year after you expressly told him that Valentine's gifts are silly, but they make you feel loved.

As the day passed without a peep from him, your heart broke. A wave of negativity hit you: why did he *insist* on hurting you like this? Why did he care so little about you? You spend all the following day feeling tearful. Why were men like this? All men have hurt you, starting from your father. What was the use? Maybe, the truth is that you don't deserve love. Maybe, love is for other women but not you. You know, because you're so broken. After all, you can tell that he now knows it was Valentine's Day, but he's just deliberately choosing to say nothing...

Can you see what's happened?

1. The trigger is like an alarm bell that feels like a threat to us and to our emotional connection

2. We each revert to our "story" about what this negativity means

3. The story triggers a wave of negative emotions

4. Those negative emotions lead to certain ingrained behavior patterns that we have learnt to use to cope. We become reactive, defensive, protective, or just shut down

5. These responses in turn become triggers for behavior in the other person

6. We keep on triggering one another, and hey presto, you have yourself an infinite argument.

Here's how that looked for our Valentine's Day fight:

The missed day triggered my "story" about how Katie was making unreasonable demands on me, getting angry with me for nothing, being materialistic and entitled, not to mention ignoring all the loving things I *did* do for her. This story about how unreasonable she was to expect things from me came from, you guessed it, my old attachment wounds (are you sick of them yet? Katie was!).

The missed day triggered Katie's "story" which was a miserable tale of her inadequacy and being abandoned when all she wanted was to be loved. In this story, there is no such thing as mere forgetfulness – my actions meant 100% total rejection, and that was absolute proof that she was, on a fundamental level, unworthy of love.

Now, with both of us nicely primed with these awful stories swimming around in our heads, our negative feelings only escalated, and we both responded in the same way we always did: I withdrew, and she despaired. The more I withdrew, the more she despaired; the more upset I saw she was, the more unreasonable she seemed to me... and the more I withdrew.

How do we break these vicious cycles of negativity?

One trick I learnt using EFT theory is that **beneath every infinite argument lies unmet attachment needs**. Buried way down under everything was my own need to be validated for everything I did do for my wife. Under her despair was an unmet need for support, attention and tenderness.

I needed her to acknowledge how hard I was already working to make her happy.

She needed me to show her love in the way that she could actually receive it.

Our needs were always legitimate. The way we went about trying to meet those needs, however, left a lot to be desired.

Neither of us could get our needs met because we didn't even know we had these needs, let alone know how to communicate them. I blamed her and she blamed me, and the more we did this the more we turned away from one another and towards our own nonsense "stories" that merely intensified negative feelings and justified that blame. We were operating from a position of fear and threat. From that place, communication is impossible.

So now what? Uncovering a vicious cycle like this one is only half the work. The other half is to consciously replace it with something better. This is what we'll be focusing on this week.

Week 3 Exercise

The previous week's tasks may have already begun to stir up difficult feelings, and you may have already gone a few rounds on your own personal "infinite argument." That's OK. What follows is a kind of roadmap for emotion-focused communication that lowers feelings of threat and negativity, while maximizing your chances of uncovering and addressing all those unmet needs.

Importantly, it's not so much *what* you say as *how* you say it. And even more important that what you say is what you hear your partner saying. I want to share one of my favorite golden rules of communication: **Listen to understand, not to respond**. To put it in blunter terms, ff you want to be a better communicator, the first step is to learn to shut up!

Active listening is not just sitting quietly while you wait for someone to stop, so you can have your turn. Listening is really a mix of many separate skills:

Reflecting – Let them know you've heard by paraphrasing. "It seems to me like you're saying…" This not only confirms your understanding but communicates that their message is worth being heard correctly.

Validating – Basically, making sure the other person feels that their emotions *make sense* and are fully legitimate. "I can see why you feel that way."

Summarizing – This doesn't mean hurrying people along, but listening closely so you can capture the essence of what's been shared with you in a succinct way. Think and express along with them.

Asking questions – The best questions are ones that demonstrate your close attention and comprehension. Ask to clarify, then reiterate and to confirm your own interpretation. Ask to demonstrate your own interest and attention.

While the above may seem easy-peasy, remember that when a negative cycle is already underway, both parties may have strong negative emotions activated. Often, these *primary emotions* (fear, sadness, anger) are hard to feel, so instead we express them in conditioned ways and they manifest as secondary emotions (irritation, defensiveness, indignation) that only make it harder for use to connect with our own emotions or theirs. We start responding in fear instead of trust, and reacting to our own stories about our loved ones rather than the people who are standing right in front of us.

When we give in to these secondary emotions, it eats away at the foundation of trust and intimacy. When we fully express our primary emotions and communicate our needs, however, we create enormous safety and connection – that's why people who use EFT principles can use arguments to actually bring them closer together.

When talking to your partner, imagine that everything they're saying is secret code for, "are you there? Do you see me? Do you accept me?" Imagine, too, that the quickest way to resolve conflict is to respond, in whatever way you can, "I'm here for you. I see you. I accept you."

This week's exercise is to practice compassionate communication with your partner, but with an emphasis on just listening. **Your goal is to listen for unmet needs**. You may even decide to schedule things so that in one meeting one talks and the other listens, and vice versa for a separate meeting at another time.

1. Take a deep breath, pause for a moment and make sure you are alone and won't be interrupted by anything.

2. Connect. Face one another, make eye contact and, if you like, connect physically with a handhold or similar. Give them your absolute attention.

3. Acknowledge your own emotions but consciously set them aside for the time being and put your partner and their feelings at center stage.

4. Invite your partner to speak, and then listen to understand, not to respond. Reflect, validate and ask questions, but mostly just be there, and hear them. Don't be afraid of silence.

5. Keep listening for emotions and needs.

6. When they feel like they've finish, try saying something like, "thank you for sharing that with me." Remember that it's not for you to decide when they're finished!

7. One optional step is to end with a moment of gratitude and appreciation. Take turns thinking of something you value in one another or recognize something positive what they've done or said.

And that's it. Simple, yes, but not always easy. When it's your turn to share, remember to keep the focus on your own emotions, rather than on the other person's actions or shortcomings. That means saying, "I feel…" rather than "you make me feel…" It's the difference between saying, "I'm sad and feel abandoned" and "*you* went and abandoned me, you a**hole!"

This is not the time for diagnosing, insulting, labeling or mind-reading. At the same time, realize that you don't have to agree with everything you hear in order to accept and acknowledge it. This can take practice. If you feel your own negative emotions arising in response to what you hear, try to see this as separate from your ability to comprehend *their* emotions on the matter. In my own example, Katie truly felt like I had deliberately chosen to hurt her. Let me tell you, all I wanted to do when she said that was jump in and argue with her – she was wrong, I loved her, and she had misunderstood.

But I had to realize that that was *my* feeling. *Her* feeling was sadness and rejection. I had to walk a narrow path: to fully accept that she felt the way she felt, and that those feelings were legitimate, even though my own feelings were so at odds with hers. To master truly effective conversation requires consciously letting these potential fuses go unlit.

What made the penny drop for me was reminding myself of my ultimate goal. I loved her and wanted our relationship to continue. So, what was more important – me "correcting" her and telling her what the facts of the situation were, or me being able to put down the weapon I was carrying and tell her, "I'm here for you. I see you. I see your feelings of sadness and rejection. I accept them. I accept you."

I can guarantee you that the feelings of vulnerability that emerge can be scary – but they're also like jet fuel for connection, and they instantly melt resistance, defensiveness and fear.

Week 4

Needs, Wants and Everything in Between

"When you're in a relationship you should never put your wants before your partner's needs." ~ Sonya Parker

By now, you and your partner should be getting a clearer picture of the central issue in your relationship. You should also be seeing a bit more deeply into automatic, negative patterns of communication between you both. No surprises here: those two things are inevitably connected.

No two couples are the same, but the dynamic between a couple will itself change over time, too. This means that there can never be a one-size-fits-all approach to communication, or a step-by-step procedure that always leads to the same guaranteed outcome. What we can work with, however, is a repeated focus on what matters: emotions.

We focus here because **emotions are connected to our needs.**

Only when two halves of a couple are able to consistently communicate their emotions, are they able to meet one another's needs. This was a revelation for me: the idea that Katie and I could actively benefit one another. It wasn't all compromise and negotiation; rather, as a couple we could be more than the sum of our parts. We could make life easier for one another. What a powerful idea!

EFT, then, is about setting up new, healthy patterns – ones that strengthen trust and connection with every cycle. It's about transforming these positive communication patterns into a little engine that generates love and joy, like a machine that gets stronger the more it runs, and easily solves the everyday problems it encounters.

We've begun to explore ways of expressing our emotions as well as hearing the expressed emotions of our partner; this week is about seeing what all this expression is *for*. We're returning to needs and wants in this module, specifically:

1. Becoming aware of your own wants and needs

2. Learning how to express them to your partner

3. Becoming aware of your partner's wants and needs

4. Jointly arrive at some new solutions, shared goals or ways forward

What we all need

Let's begin with the basics, however. What does every human being alive need?

To phrase this a little differently, why do any of us enter into romantic relationships at all? Despite their obvious drawbacks and difficulties, despite our gaps in emotional intelligence, and despite the many risks and costs, most of us will repeatedly attempt to connect with another soul. Why?

Human beings are built for connection. We are born small and helpless, and for the first years of our lives, our wellbeing is nothing more than the degree to which we can rest in the warmth and love of our mothers. As we grow, our relationships with others change, and what we need from others changes, too, but relationships are always there, at the core of our experience.

Without friends, family, partners, and social connections of all kinds, it's hard to imagine what a human being even is.

So, we'll start there: each and every one of us *needs* to be in relationship. Not necessarily romantic relationship, of course, but some sense that we are connected in a meaningful way to our social reality. When we are babies, our mothers look into our faces and behold us. We feel seen. We feel our own existence for the first time; we understand, from that moment, that we are individuals, but also that there are other individuals out there. And that suddenly means that there are possibilities for connection and interaction. We cry or laugh and observe our mother respond to us – *it is in her reaction to our emotion* that we begin to understand what we feel, what we want. Who we are. Other people, then, are mirrors.

In every relationship, all human beings need:

- To be seen and heard – understood and recognized as unique individuals in their own right

- To be connected to their world, i.e. to be a part of something

- To have the opportunity to contribute meaningfully to that world

- To feel respected, safe and free from harm

- To have a sense of identity, meaning and purpose

- To be able to grow, change and evolve – this includes being wrong sometimes or changing their mind

Consider this a basic "Bill of Emotional Human Rights." You might have noticed a few things that are *not* on the list – I have not included the "need" to always be right, to be superior, to win, to experience eternal comfort and ease, to be flattered or coddled. I have not even listed love as a need – nor sex, for that matter. The above needs are fundamental to *all* relationships; if even one is missing, you have a serious problem on your hands.

I'm beginning with these needs because, sadly, many of us are in relationships where we have come to believe that we're not entitled to very much, and are far too willing to compromise on some or all of the above. Let me assure you – you are entitled to all of them. No questions asked.

That said, being a human being and relating to others then automatically implies that *you* provide the same rights for your fellow humans. Again, if you are consistently denying someone close to you any of the above, you have a serious problem on your hands. Now you can see the flip side of things: you are never compelled to love someone, but you should always, always make sure that you are supplying them with respect, understanding and the freedom to be who they actually are.

What YOU need

So those are the needs we all have by default, just by virtue of being a human being. Of course, one big part of being human is how different we all are, and with this comes variation in how important certain needs are, relatively speaking.

On our journey, for example, Katie and I discovered that I had a far more pronounced need for alone time and privacy than she did. Oh, she needed it alright, just never as much as I did.

On the other hand, it was extremely important for Katie to feel like I had heard and understood her when she was expressing something important to her. I never much needed this validation, but I soon learnt that Katie had a greater need for this kind of mirroring from those around her than I would have ever guessed.

I would say that a full 25% of all of our misunderstandings and arguments came simply from not recognizing that each of us had slightly different needs. It was in fact Katie that helped me better understand this. One day we were in the kitchen and taking our multivitamins. Curious, she grabbed the bottles and compared the labels. Hers contained slightly less of every vitamin (which made sense given she weighed 30lb. less than I did) but way more iron (for obvious reasons). "Look at this" she said, "if we have slightly different needs when it comes to vitamins, why shouldn't we have different needs in all other areas, too?"

It may seem pretty obvious when you put it this way, but how many of us are looking for *consensus* when it comes to needs, rather than acknowledging that each of us requires something a little different to feel happy and healthy in their relationship? I'll address men specifically here, since we have a tendency to assume that if *we* don't have a particular need, then the existence of that need in our partners is somehow not really legitimate. I've heard many men dismiss their wives' pleas for more closeness simply because they themselves don't have that need.

The fact that Katie needed more iron than I did wasn't a problem — she didn't have to take less to be like me, and I didn't have to take more to be like her. In the same way, we never needed to argue about what the "right" amount of alone time for a person should be, or how much talking was enough – she needed one amount, and I needed another.

Now, if you're smart, I bet your mind is rushing ahead to the natural conclusion of this line of thought. "If Katie needs to talk a lot, but you don't, then how can you both possibly get your needs met?" Well, this is an excellent observation, and the entire reason we explore needs when it comes to couples' therapy.

No human being is compelled to meet all the needs of another human being (except, perhaps, for the mother of a newborn, but that's another story). When we get together into a relationship with someone, however, we are agreeing to mutually meet some of one another's needs. Which needs? How much do we meet them?

Finding the answers to those questions is the work of every individual couple – and it's often work that needs to be revisited again and again. Remember what I said about there being no one-size-fits-all solutions? This is precisely what I was getting at. Each couple decides between them how to mutually (joyfully!) fulfil the others' needs, within reason. If they do this well, the relationship is successful. If not, well, you know how it goes.

For me and Katie, the happy compromise comes in this form: she has a lot more friends and acquaintances than I do, and she spends a lot more time socializing with them. This way, although she does connect with me, she fulfils her extra need for connection by spending quality time with others. Simultaneously, this leaves me with plenty of quiet time to myself, where I can recharge and get the privacy I want. We didn't resolve our difference in needs by forcing us both to accept a compromise that didn't really suit either of us (that would be like averaging the total amount of iron and then dividing it equally between us). Instead, we used honest, loving communication to find a practical solution that ensured we were both getting our needs met.

In this week's exercise, we are going to simply focus on identifying our personal needs, then expressing them to our partners. How we negotiate their fulfilment is a task for another day, but before we continue, bear in mind a few key points for communicating needs:

- Both you and your partner are entitled to the needs in the Bill of Emotional Human Rights given above. These are the non-negotiables.

- Needs and wants beyond this *are* negotiable. Note I say "negotiate" and not bully, demand, intimidate, coerce and so on. There is a careful balance between needs, wants and boundaries. It's OK to explore this balance. That's how you find a solution that works.

- Remind yourself that just because you have a need or want, it does not entitle you to having it met *by your partner*. Your need does not automatically become an obligation for your partner. Nor should you feel that you have to meet their needs just because they express them.

- Finally, be alert for unreasonable demands that are dressed up as needs. We cannot, for example, have a need that our partner be someone they're not, or one that requires them to relinquish one of their needs.

Week 4 Exercise

Take turns expressing your needs and emotions to your partner.

Remember, for now you are not making demands or requests – you are simply expressing your emotional reality, and listening compassionately as they express their emotional reality. You are not placing orders or making demands on their behavior.

Experiment with the following format:

I have a need for _____.

When that need is met, I feel _____.

When that need is not met, I feel _____.

Go through each emotional need you may have, and perhaps take some time exploring which ones are most important, and which are more wants than needs. Are there any differences between you and your partner?

Finally, end this exercise by sharing one way in which you already feel that your partner is meeting your needs, and how. Express gratitude.

Noah and Billie

Noah and Billie sailed through the exercises on relationship goals – that's because they are exactly on the same page and want the same things from life and from one another. However, with this exercise they were stunned to discover that this shared goal would actually be meeting a very different need in each of them, and this has important consequences for how they communicate and resolve conflict.

Both Noah and Billie have dreams of career success, buying a house together and filling that house with kids and dogs. They've even spoken at length about going into certain business ventures together. Noah, however, has a strong need for independence and the freedom to make his own way, whereas Billie's primary need is to belong, to feel safe and secure as she builds a family. While both see their relationship as meeting their respective needs, they're now much more aware of just how different their approaches are. This opened a world of unspoken assumptions and expectations they were oblivious to before – and helped them understand one another a whole lot more.

Week 5

Building Emotional Intimacy

"A friend is someone who knows the song in your heart and can sing it back to you when you have forgotten the words." ~ Donna Roberts

If you're anything like me, the word "intimacy" is a little cringe-inducing. However, it's also a label for one of the most important qualities of any healthy relationship. Mastering intimacy is one of those skills you may wonder how you ever survived without. First things first: intimacy is not about sex. It's not physical at all. We'll define intimacy here as *emotional closeness.*

Intimacy is not about chemistry or how well you like one another. Rather, its ingredients are:

- Trust

- Empathy

- Vulnerability

By looking more closely at the three elements that make up intimacy, we can see exactly how to create more of it.

Trust. You don't instantly trust just anyone. It takes time to build confidence and faith in someone else, and it takes time to build intimacy. You don't trust someone because of what they say, but what they do… that's why trust and intimacy are a result of repeated actions that demonstrate your trustworthiness, dependability and safety to your partner.

Empathy. To empathize means to see deeply into someone else's emotional world. To feel what they feel. To understand, to care and to value without judgment. This too is something that builds over time, and with conscious actions that protect and support that sympathetic understanding.

Vulnerability. This one's arguably the secret sauce in the intimacy recipe, and it's tricky to define. Basically, to be vulnerable means to be exposed to such a degree that one might incur damage or loss. It's an act of opening up to someone in such a way that it would cost you if the other person abused that special access you've granted them.

Now, I want to say a few things about these ingredients. Firstly, you'll notice something they all have in common: they take *time*, and they are based on consciously chosen *action*. Intimacy here is not just a warm fuzzy feeling you get for free – it's a sate to deliberately and effortfully cultivate (sexy, right?). That means to build intimacy requires not only consistent action, but enough patience over time to allow the fruits of that action to grow.

What's more, each of these components inspires the other. If you are vulnerable and open up to another person, and they respect and honor that vulnerability, it builds trust. In that trust, you can begin to empathize. The more empathy there is, the easier it is to open further and be even more vulnerable. We can conclude, then, that intimacy is actually a process – it's a positive feedback loop that gradually grows and strengthens in a healthy relationship.

Getting an intimacy baseline reading

Where are you and your partner right now?

If we take intimacy to simply mean "emotional closeness" then where do you both fall, on a scale of one to ten?

How much would you say you trust your partner right now? How much do they trust you?

How easy is it for you both to empathize with one another? How much compassion and understanding is there?

Finally, how ready do each of you feel to be vulnerable with the other?

Answering these questions can give you a fairly accurate estimate of the overall total intimacy or closeness you're both currently experiencing in the relationship. One of the things that opened my eyes to the need for change in my own relationship was just how different Katie's rating was from mine. I thought we were pretty close, but from her perspective, we were basically estranged.

We talked a long time about the issue, and my ego took a pretty big blow to discover that she didn't feel much trust in me. I couldn't understand it – I had always been faithful, I had never lied to her, I was an honest man, wasn't I? As you can see, I didn't yet understand that what was missing was *emotional* trust.

As we discussed things further, and I listened empathetically, I learnt that Katie's lack of trust came from a deeper feeling that I just wasn't on her side. She saw me repeatedly choosing to prioritize myself and my own wants over hers, sometimes just plain forgetting to consider her. It wasn't that she thought I was untrustworthy exactly; it was more that she was not entirely convinced that I was 100% there for her. When she'd ask to talk or she'd reach out and look for reassurance, sometimes she'd get it. But sometimes I'd brush her off or dismiss her bid for attention. In other words, she could not trust me with her emotions.

As time went on, we discovered, to her shock and mine, that I didn't trust her all that much either. We had spent so long negotiating her emotional needs and my eternal failure to meet them that we scarcely paid attention to whether I felt safe enough to be vulnerable. Like far too many men, I floated along with the assumption that tenderness and compassion and intimacy and warmth and all those lovely things were what I needed to supply to *her*. I scarcely allowed myself to acknowledge that somehow, both Katie and I had made the unconscious agreement that I was not really allowed to be vulnerable. Sure, I was allowed to be angry, or demanding, or cold, or distant. But if I ever willingly exposed my weakness or vulnerability, Katie would subtly recoil. It eroded my trust in her.

Of course, none of this is easy to share, but the differences between men and women when it comes to intimacy are worth dwelling on. If intimacy is a product of the ability to be vulnerable, and we live in a culture that is happy to permit women a degree of vulnerability they don't grant to men, then we cannot be too surprised when men are less willing, or less able, to demonstrate intimacy. The way forward is not for women to demand more intimacy from men, but for women to give men the same conditions of trust, vulnerability and empathy that they themselves require to feel close.

I'm the first to admit that I've been the annoying "strong, silent type" who keeps his emotions to himself; but the more I learn, the more I see that this is just one side of the coin. The other side is how, culturally, we don't make space for men to be emotional. Too many couples (heterosexual ones, anyway) practice a kind of emotional division of labor – the women do the bulk of it, and the men begrudgingly do a little, too. But for all those male readers out there, I want to shout it from the rooftops: emotions are not "women's work"! For women, I offer a gentle reminder that the men in your life are capable of just as much uncertainty, fear, weakness, vulnerability, shame, confusion and loss as you are.

Baby steps

Intimacy is something you can only build gradually. The more distance between you, the more time it will take to cover that distance, step by step. If we wish to build more intimacy with our partners, we need to start thinking of our sense of closeness with them almost like a bank account. The more you invest in this account over time, the more interest you earn, and the more it grows. A full account can withstand a knock to trust here and there – a "withdrawal" – but if the account is already close to empty, there may be nothing to give.

When you keep your promises, when you help your partner feel safe, when you honor and cherish their vulnerability when it's shared with you, it's like making a tiny deposit into the account. It takes a while to build that up, but once you've built it, it's not going anywhere. If you and your partner hit a rough patch, you have this accumulated store of trust you've built together to fall back on.

I want to tell you about a couple I know, however. They too found themselves in couples' therapy, after she discovered his repeated affairs. They hit rock bottom, and so did their trust account. In fact, the trust account was overdrawn. To his credit, he was repentant and got to work winning her back. He kept his promises, he did whatever he could to make her feel safe, and he took active steps to protect their relationship, which was now on life-support.

In a few months, though, things were still rocky. He had stopped the affairs, and she had forgiven him. The problem was more subtle, however. Though he was doing everything right, the account was seriously overdrawn – it would take a long time for them to build that balance up again. My friend's mistake was to assume that he had any trust stored in his account at all. He wanted to be closer to her, and to move on, and grew impatient with how hesitant she was being. He couldn't understand why she was being so cold and aloof with him. He didn't get it: he was in trust debt.

This is an extreme example, but it's worth remembering that when it comes to trust and intimacy, there are no sudden moves. It takes time. Intimacy is not something that magically appears in your world simply because you've decided you'd like it to. For couples whose relationships have become a bit rocky, this can feel like a catch-22. There may be a loss of trust and therefore a drop in intimacy, but the only way you can build more intimacy is if you trust each other more. And you just don't.

So, how on earth do you get out of trust debt? The answer is baby steps. Teeny, tiny baby steps.

Week 5 Exercise

This week, the goal is to start making those tiny investments in one another again. Depending on the current balance in your trust account, you may have a short way to go, or you may have some serious rebuilding to do. Either way, intimacy will be repaired one bit at a time. Here's exactly how that looks:

1. One or both of you takes a baby step towards one another (i.e. more closeness).

2. That closeness is maintained without breaking trust.

The result is a feeling of warmth and empathy that makes it a tiny bit easier to do the process again. This process is *tiny*, however. You may share your feelings and open up a little (step 1) and your partner listens, reflects back without judgment, and genuinely tries to understand your perspective (step 2). Or perhaps someone takes a tiny leap of faith and sets a boundary (step 1). The other respects that boundary and doesn't make it "cost" anything (step 2). One final example is if someone takes responsibility and apologizes in earnest (step 1). The other person receives this and forgives, without using it as a weapon for retaliation or revenge (step 2).

You get the idea. This week, see how many little steps you can try and take towards your partner (not big, risky leaps – just baby steps) and in turn see how you can reward the steps they take with acceptance, empathy, kindness and respect.

Jay and Nathalie

I'll let Jay explain it: "Nathalie and I almost finished things. We pulled through, but she told me in no uncertain terms: this would be a new relationship. The old one had broken. So, I invited her out – I told her it would be our first date. No foregone conclusions, no expectations, no assumptions. If we were going to start again, then I wanted to do it for real. I can tell you something, I have never been more nervous about a date in my life!"

Week 6

Forgiveness and Healing

"I saw that you were perfect, and so I loved you. Then I saw that you were not perfect and I loved you even more." ~ Angelita Lim

This week, I'm going to take a few tentative steps toward a topic that has been, let's be honest, simmering just beneath the surface of things.

"Sure, I hear what you're saying about communication and vulnerability and emotions and all that jazz. That all sounds great. It's just… you don't understand what he/she has *done*. I'm the good guy here, trying to get over what the bad guy did to me. Things aren't so simple!"

My advice here is advice that I myself was given once: when you find yourself saying things like, "it's not that simple" it's almost always evidence of something unforgiven. Some sign of incomplete healing. A little sore spot on your heart. More obviously, if one or both parties in a couple is framing the interaction in terms of good guy vs. bad guy, victim vs. perpetrator or guilty vs. innocent, no progress can be made until that frame is dissolved.

A big clue here: it's dissolved not when everyone finds out for sure who the bad guy, perpetrator or guilty one really is, so their punishment can be meted out. It's dissolved only when that distance between good guy and bad guy is closed. Remembering that intimacy is closeness, it's easy to see why unhealed wounds and unforgiven deeds will always remain an obstacle to connection and intimacy. What's more, the path forward will also seem more obvious: it's forgiveness and healing.

The ground we're about to tread can be extremely hazardous. Nowhere will your own inbuilt attachment patterns become more obvious than in the realm where you feel wronged, aggrieved or cheated. Furthermore, we can also find our old negative core beliefs fearsomely triggered by the sense that *we* may be the bad guy in the picture, or at least recognize that we're being perceived that way.

This week we are doing the difficult work of processing and moving on from wounds, old and new, and allowing that healing to guide the way we move forward with our partners. We will look at both sides – i.e. the art of not just forgiving our partner but also of asking for and receiving their forgiveness (admit it, you probably started this chapter with the assumption that we'd focus on the former more than the latter, right? Imagine if everyone got into the habit of doing the opposite).

Let's start putting together a theory of forgiveness – what it is, what it isn't, and how to do it. In the EFT framework for couples, we put emotional intimacy at the center. We prioritize self-awareness paired with communication, and we jointly learn to set goals that allow both to have their needs met, given their unique attachment styles and, shall we say, "baggage."

From this perspective, forgiveness is not a brave, self-effacing move that you do to prove that you're the bigger person. It's not something you *have to* do, and it's also not something you're entitled to receive from anyone. Rather, forgiveness in this context can be understood as a **corrective**. So far, we've covered plenty of ground on healthy communication, listening, sharing and all that good stuff. But the truth is we are all human, and we all fall short of whatever ideal we set for ourselves, sooner or later. Even in the best-case scenario we may hurt those we love, either by accident or simply because of our own weakness and fallibility.

This is what forgiveness is for – *to allow us to be imperfectly human and nevertheless stay on the path*. Forgiveness allows us to preserve what is good and worth keeping, while gently making space for what is difficult so that there is a chance it can be redeemed, learnt from, or healed. In today's world, people are more intolerant of one another than ever before, and can become hypersensitive to the tiniest transgressions, especially if we've been hurt before. We may be so unable to tolerate grey-areas and imperfection that we'd rather ditch an entire relationship than work through a very human-sized "red flag."

Though it may not seem like it, forgiveness and healing are often the easier way through. They're connected, too – it's those things we are unable to forgive in ourselves and others that haunt us and keep us unhappy. It's ironically the things that we surrender to, let go of and accept that are the most likely to leave us in peace.

I understand the kinds of burning questions and objections that fill a wounded heart: *why should I have to do the work of forgiving when they are the one that did the Bad Thing? What about if a transgression is too big to forgive? How will I know if this is a growth opportunity or just a warning sign to run and never look back? How can I forgive someone who doesn't think they've done anything wrong?*

These are all valid questions. To go some of the way to answering them (doing them justice would require a book ten times the length of this one, so I'll be brief) I want to share two examples below from couples we met during our EFT course days. Both are stories of forgiveness, but they look very, very different.

There are many ways to heal

The first couple were childhood sweethearts who grew up together. From the beginning neither wanted children, but after two decades together, the woman found herself changing her mind. Her desire to be a mother grew until the couple were forced to have some difficult conversations. He felt blindsided and as though she had suddenly changed the "contract." She knew all this but couldn't help what she wanted – time had marched on, she had changed, and along the way so had her needs.

The two thrashed it out for years, trying to find a way through. There wasn't one. It was clear that sooner or later, they'd have to end things, despite loving one another enormously and having never even considered that their futures might not be spent together. He grew to resent what felt like a bait-and-switch. She grew to resent his inflexibility, and how he seemingly chose to see her as a deceiver rather than someone who had just evolved. The two were trapped together, him unable to let go of his resentment, her unable to let go of hers.

For this couple, healing, forgiveness and growth took the form of breaking up.

The two released one another with as much kindness and compassion as they could muster. They forgave one another not for this or that transgression, but for the bigger sin of simply being human, being changeable, and being different from one another. They forgave the unfairness of the world, the tragedy of their story, the randomness of fate… they forgave it all. And that forgiveness was what allowed them to stop keeping certain wounds open, so they could both move on.

I'll tell you something, I have never seen two people navigate a breakup with as much grace and maturity as they did. They are friends to this day, and even though they're much younger than me, I see them as role models.

The other couple had the more classic story of wrongdoing and forgiveness. He had an anger problem and one day, in the heat of the moment, slapped her. Their world came apart. She had always had one firm rule: she would never, ever tolerate physical abuse of any kind. It was a total dealbreaker. Yet when faced with that unthinkable outcome, neither could bear ending what had been a long and mostly happy relationship.

Despite urging from everyone around her to leave and never look back, and despite her own considerable hurt and doubt, she forgave him. Not because he deserved it or because she agreed with what he'd done. She forgave him because there was an appalling chasm of distance that had opened between them and forgiving him was the one thing she could do to *correct* that, and bring them closer again. Yes, he was the one that had first introduced that distance by his profound act of disrespect and violence. But she knew that she would only maintain and add to that distance by holding onto his crime and allowing that to define their relationship forever.

I'm not saying whether she was right or wrong. That's really for her to decide. But she laid down the law for him: she would take an enormous leap of faith back towards him and place an impossibly huge vote of confidence in him and their relationship... but she would only do it once. He heard that. The size of her forgiveness became the size of his contrition. He knew, too, that making excuses or feeling sorry for himself would only get in the way. Instead, he made it his life's mission to make sure her forgiveness mean something. Her forgiveness was an investment in their relationship, and he would do whatever he could to match and exceed that investment.

I share these two stories to make a few points clear. Forgiveness is not about "saving" a relationship. Healing could end it, change it, or start it completely anew. Forgiveness is more like a reckoning and balancing of the books. For some couples, healing might look like calling it a day; for others it may look like the start of a stronger, better relationship. Forgiveness isn't about the outcome; it's about *how* you process certain events and shortcomings.

What if your partner has done something truly unforgiveable? Well, if a relationship is fundamentally flawed, then it will end, one way or another. But forgiveness in this case means something more general: it means letting go of these flaws, forgiving ourselves, forgiving the situation for not being what we wanted, forgiving the impossibility of it all, and finding a way to move forward with compassion and acceptance.

For most couples, though, things are seldom this dire. In fact, I've noticed that the initial pain of forgiveness and letting go is far easier than we predict it will be. If we are willing to forgive one another's imperfections and respond instead to a genuine and heartfelt desire to connect, and to keep connecting despite getting it wrong now and again, then forgiveness and healing becomes an everyday thing. It becomes something we want to do.

I forgive my wife a dozen times a day, and she does the same for me. It's necessary relationship hygiene, like housework.

Week 6 Exercise

There are two exercises we'll do this week.

The first is done individually. You and your partner are to separately keep journals where you write down your thoughts, feelings and reflections about the wounds you feel you may have gathered up in the course of your relationship. This is not so much an exercise in blame or attacking your partner, but rather a gentle and honest accounting of where you may be feeling wounded right now.

Think in terms of how these wounds have impacted your ability to be *close* to your partner. What is stopping this wound from healing? What would you need and want to feel ready to let go of this? More seriously, does this wound hold the key to a truth that you may have been avoiding? Have we communicated our feelings about this wound before?

Sometimes our partners hurt us because they're only human, and, like we ourselves, they are not always perfectly kind and considerate. Sometimes, though, the wound comes from a deeper misalignment of values or goals. Healing may begin when you are able to look honestly and compassionately at these more serious wounds and what they mean for you as a couple.

When you have both spent some time processing individually, it's time to bring that insight into connection with one another. Write a letter to your partner, where you kindly but honestly express the current condition of your heart, and the wounds you find there. Focus on describing your own feelings, rather than their crimes and faults. In the same letter express, in your own unique way, any desire you hold to find more closeness, and close the gap between you both. If you feel you'd like to, ask for their forgiveness and understanding for everything you could have done better.

Lizzie and Ben

One afternoon, Ben had a near-death experience when his car was nearly demolished by an eighteen-wheeler truck. He describes how, in that instant, he felt an unbearably strong impulse to reach out to Lizzie. He called her at once, breathless, and blurted, "Please forgive me. I forgive you. I love you. I'm sorry." All the grievances that had passed between them vanished utterly; in that moment he only wanted one thing: to be close to her.

Week 7

Building Trust

"You may be deceived if you trust too much, but you will live in torment unless you trust enough." ~ Frank Crane

Congratulations – you have now made it passed the halfway mark of the twelve-week program. How about a quick check-in?

- Recalling the relationship goals you initially set as a couple, consider your progress over the last few weeks. Have your goals changed at all? What has worked well and what are you still grappling with?

- You've been challenged to reach out to your partner and communicate with them in ways that may feel unfamiliar or even risky. What aspects of communication do you feel are getting stronger, and what aspects still need some attention?

- How would you and your partner rate your overall sense of intimacy, and how well do you feel like your needs are currently being met?

- Finally, last week may have been a heavy one – where are you now with your own healing? How did it feel to open in vulnerability to your partner and share some of this?

This week, as we move into the second half of the program, I want to switch gears a little. Relationship work and EFT-style exercises can be daunting and emotionally fraught, there's no doubt about it. But for now, I want to draw attention to the fact that relationships are also supposed to be *fun*. Yes, it's easy to forget this if you've been toiling too long in the couples' therapy trenches!

Connecting with another human being is something we do because, on the deepest level possible, it feels good. When we connect, we feel whole, alive, witnessed. The world seems right, we feel braver and kinder than we thought we ever could be, and we discover something else amazing: that we can be the source of someone else's joy and meaning. What I'm saying is that we wouldn't submit to all this hard work if there wasn't some point to it all.

We go through the slog of improving our communication and owning our baggage and healing and forgiving and all of that not because we ought to or because it's a kind of chore, like just one more thing on our To Do list. We do it because *it feels so good to connect*. Because we want to. Because nothing in the world feels better than real intimacy with someone we adore, and who adores us.

That's why this week we're focusing on building trust, but framing it as an exercise in *voluntary, pleasurable submission*. Bear with me on this. Trusting our partners can sometimes feel like flinging ourselves out of an airplane, right? But think of it this way – there are people who skydive on purpose because of how utterly thrilling it is. Trusting in another person expands your boundaries, gives you a sense of freedom and expansiveness, and can feel genuinely exciting.

When we discussed attachment styles, you may have noticed that the theme of trust runs deep through human attachment. The helpless infant is unable to do anything but trust their primary caregivers, and the world in general. Think about that state of mind for a moment – the feeling of knowing that your entire life and wellbeing are resting in the hands of another (almost certainly flawed) person.

Imagine it now. Imagine that everything you have is a gift from someone who has made the effort to show you care and compassion. Every pain and discomfort you are spared is solely because someone deliberately thought about your needs, and took pains to protect you. You have no defenses. Your experience is almost entirely mediated by the kindness and attention of those around you.

As you read this, you might think, "wow, how terrifying!"

But there is another way to think of this radical trust and submission: "Oh, how utterly luxurious! How relaxing to be so loved and taken care of!"

The exercise I'll share below is a lot of fun, but it's also a very powerful way to work at that fundamental level where our initial experiences of trust in others were set down. For those with insecure attachment, it can be very hard to think of vulnerability and submission as welcome or pleasurable. If we are avoidant, we may feel like we're the only ones in the world we can trust. If we're fearful avoidant, we might trust nobody, ourselves included!

Building trust with your partner is a way to gently shift these old patterns and assumptions you inherited from childhood. What's more, it's the realm where we discover a whole world of playfulness, warmth, fun and flirtation. I have no studies to back this up, but I strongly suspect that a couple who cannot have fun with one another is a couple who don't fully trust one another.

Week 7 Exercise

Let's try a fun trust-building exercise (I sound like one of those corporate team-building types, don't I?). The game is one you've probably already played as a child. It goes like this: one of you is blindfolded, and the other one takes charge of guiding them around some mildly hazardous course. The task itself builds trust and can be quite entertaining, but it's also worth paying attention to what this demands of your communication, your connection and your empathy with one another.

The principle is obvious. One person is essentially saying, "come with me... you can trust me" and the other is invited to do just that. Naturally, you don't want to pick a terrain where any serious harm could befall either of you, but at the same time, you do want to go some way to recreating that helpless infant state of mind we discussed earlier.

One variation on this game includes doing a blindfolded walk outside. Take turns putting on the blindfold, and then walk straight while your partner stands beside you, using their voice to guide you safely on. Using their voice alone will challenge them to communicate clearly and with empathy, while it will challenge you to practice trusting those words. Guiding while using touch or a handhold introduces a different element and slightly different challenges.

Another variation is to conduct some other simple activity while wearing the blindfold. This could be spending an hour with it on and simply moving around the house doing ordinary things with your partner's guidance, or a specific task like eating, getting dressed or checking the mailbox. Each variation is fun/challenging in a slightly different way, but each one hinges on the real experience of trust – both creating it for your partner, and relaxing into it yourself. It really is up to you how you'd like to experiment!

Trust = vulnerability = connection

I wanted to share a few interesting stories about couples who have tried the above exercise, and their experiences with deliberately cultivating trust in such a fundamental way. I'll let them explain things in their own words:

Becky

"I never would have said that James and I had any problems with trust or anything, but I was surprised how hard it was for me to let go as he was guiding me all around the house. My entire body went tense, and I was frantically feeling everywhere with my feet and hands, only inching forward a little at a time.

He said to me, 'you're not really trusting me, though – just trust me!' I actively tried to relax my body. It was the strangest sensation. I wanted to see if I could completely let go, instead of 'bracing' myself the way I had been. It was an aha moment: I realized that I trusted James, but not fully. I was walking around our relationship letting him guide me, so to speak, but all the while I was tense and fearful. I think I've always assumed that it's just easier and better to do everything myself, and I think that's made me unable to see all the ways that he is there for me, and wants to have my trust.

Funnily enough, James seems to trust me way more than I trust him! We decided to set ourselves some homework tasks. Once a week I give up control and he does something to surprise me — then I just let him. He picks an outing or an activity or he cooks me dinner or whatever. I trust that he has my best interests at heart, and that he's got my back. Actually, it's quite freeing not to have to always second-guess him. Growing up, I had pretty neglectful parents, and I think I learnt early on not to expect too much of other people. But James is slowly convincing me that some people do deserve to have our trust, and that we can safely rely on them to be there for us."

Joe

"My girlfriend and I did the walking version of this exercise, and it was hilarious. I really feel like it helped bring us much closer together. We ended up having an interesting conversation about trust, and I shared how I had been cheated on in the past, and so my trust in other people was pretty much zero. As we walked through the woods (we brought the dog — he thought it was loads of fun) I was suddenly struck by an idea. It occurred to me that in life both of us are blindfolded, in a way, and that we are both trying to guide and encourage one another along.

If we both have our eyes open, we can just easily barge ahead, independent. But blindfolded, we had to TOUCH one another. We had to connect and be close. We had to figure out a way to communicate. I was really struck by that image of my girlfriend clinging onto my arm. Truth be told, I feel as though I cling to her in just the same way! Maybe that's OK. I've always hated this idea of needing anyone, anything. It feels risky and stupid. But looking at my girlfriend's face as she reached out for my hand, I didn't really feel that way anymore. Maybe people need to need one another. I'm not sure, but we're keeping the conversation going."

When you do a trust exercise with your partner, are you, like Joe, struck by any unexpected observations? Is anything surprising to you? Do you and your partner have different feelings around trust and vulnerability? Be curious about how your own attachment style might manifest in your ability to trust your partner, and how theirs may influence their ability to trust you. It's amazing how such a simple exercise has deep roots into so many other areas of the heart and mind.

A couple that wished to stay anonymous confided in me that this exercise had triggered an unexpected rekindling of their sex life. Though I had never linked these two ideas myself, it made sense the more I thought about it. In EFT we talk at length about emotional trust, emotional vulnerability and emotional connection. But of course, as human beings, the emotional is inextricably connected to the sexual and the physical… not to mention the mental, the social, even the spiritual. What this couple discovered was a need to restore a more primal sense of trust in one another. This leads us neatly to our next module, where we will look at techniques for building romantic connection, and what that really means in the context of our unique relationships.

Week 8

Rekindling the Romance

"Absence diminishes mediocre passions and increases great ones, as the wind extinguishes candles and fans fires."
~ Francois de La Rochefoucauld

After Katie and I had spent more than two months working on our EFT course, we started to relax a little – while the ship was still adrift at sea, so to speak, the big storm felt like it was over. For the most part, we had learnt to start seeing the battle as *us versus the problem*, rather than *me versus her*. We were still unsure and unsteady about so much, but at least we knew a way forward now. At least we had tried something different and, hope against hope, it seemed to be working.

There was one thing nagging at the back of my mind, however. Katie and I would have our heart-to-heart conversations, and we'd complete our worksheets, and we'd journal, and we'd do all the things the experts say to do. It worked – I felt my love, respect and compassion for her explode. But I'll be honest, while all these warm fuzzy feelings felt safe and happy, what they didn't feel was exciting.

Katie and I were discovering what many couples in long term relationships discover, i.e. that there seems to be an inverse relationship between closeness and *attraction*. For the longest time, I couldn't understand it, and quietly admonished myself for having doubts. I thought, "your wife is happy, there's more trust and communication between you than ever before… who cares if it's not exactly the sexiest thing that's ever happened?"

In time I was better able to put my feelings into words (which was something I was getting lots of practice doing!) and I shared all this with Katie. To my surprise, she agreed with me. All this closeness, all this intimacy – it was great. It also seemed to zap every last bit of mystery and sex appeal from our connection. It was a conundrum.

My answer came not from conventional therapy circles, but rather from the ancient mystical principle that states, "the descent is for the sake of the ascent." The darkness is what helps define the light, the problem is there to help us find the solution. To put it another way, distance is the thing that makes it possible for us to attain closeness.

The more I contemplated the puzzle we found ourselves in, the more I started to understand the eternal irony of human relationships. Katie and I had done everything we could to bring us closer – that is, to create more intimacy. We drew near, we opened our hearts, we communicated on a deep level, and we connected.

But then what?

Think about the last time you felt totally, helplessly *attracted* to someone. Maybe you caught their eye across a crowded room. Maybe you caught yourself counting down the days to your next meeting, or the next phone call. Every time you weren't with them, all you could think about was being with them again. The pull was magnetic, I'm sure.

If you take two magnets, however, and bring them close together, so that there's no space between them, that magnetic pull, that irresistible force, isn't really there anymore. It doesn't have to be. You are together. In other words, when you are already with the one you're craving, you don't need to crave them quite so much anymore. You may really enjoy being together with them, but this is not the same as that electric, yearning magnetism of wanting to be together.

Katie once asked me, "how come you never write me love letters anymore?" and for a moment I felt a little guilty. The answer was obvious, though – I didn't need to. We lived together. She knew how much I loved her because I told her every day. Love letters are for those lovers who are separated, and Katie and I were very, very close.

One day we were walking home from a visit we'd taken to her parents, and all at once, Katie rushed over, picked up a big pile of dried leaves from somebody's front yard, dunked them over my head and ran away laughing. She disappeared behind a corner like a naughty child. It was completely out of character for her, but there I was, laughing all the same and chasing after her. By the time I caught her she was rosy-cheeked and gasping for breath, giggling, with bits of dried leaf tangled in her beautiful hair. Ladies and gentlemen, I could have ravished here there and then.

I'm sure you understand what I'm saying: just as the descent is for the sake of the ascent, the separation is for the sake of the reunion.

That day I understood all at once that if I wanted to bring a little spark and romance to our relationship, I would do so not by increasing the sense of closeness even further, but by creating distance. By bringing in a little more mystery, a little uncertainty, a little danger, even. Perhaps Katie had understood this long before I did, when she quite literally ran off and put some playful distance between us.

Attraction is only possible if there is a little space between you. A space where anything can happen, and there are no foregone conclusions, no routines, no guaranteed outcomes. It really is like a game of catch or hide and seek – it's only fun if for at least a portion of the game someone is hiding, or else just out of reach. You cannot play hide and seek if the other person is never out of your sight, just like you cannot flirt with someone and convince them to come back to your place if, well, they already live with you.

This is my long-winded way of saying that if you're feeling the absence of a certain spark in your relationship, then the answer may not be to get closer, but to introduce some playful distance. Absence makes the heart grow fonder, as they used to say.

Create a little gap between you – because it's that much more fun to find ways to close it again. I completely believe that a healthy relationship is one where a couple knows how to remain dynamic and limber. Let there be some spaces between you. Find a rhythm a little like breathing: sometimes you draw in close to one another, really close, and sometimes you pull right back again and get some fresh air and space. Eventually, from within that space, you start to feel the growing desire to draw back close to one another again, and the rhythm repeats. Unless you draw back, however, you never give yourself the opportunity to crave your partner in this way. You can never want them because they're never far enough away for you to experience their absence.

Pull back the catapult...

The kind of distance we want to create is that juicy, magnetic distance. You know the kind. A distance that feels buzzing and ripe with potential energy, almost like a tightly coiled up spring ready to shoot into the air, or the band of a catapult pulled pack, straining for release. The greater the distance that catapult band is pulled back, the more forceful the "reunion"!

That's the theory, but how do you realistically create this distance? Katie and I lived together, we shared the chores, we had kids and a school run and day jobs and a mortgage that needed to be paid. We had one bathroom. Not much room to create a little romantic distance, right?

Well, we just had to be creative. New relationships enjoy a degree of raw potential energy for free; after that, however, that energy needs to be deliberately cultivated if you don't want it to sputter out. It doesn't matter what you end up doing; what matters is that you don't get too comfortable taking your partner or their presence for granted. There are a few ways to do this.

Create physical distance

Literally spend some time apart. You don't have to do everything together. Spare a thought for the kind of time you're spending, too. Often, couples who spend a lot of time together are not truly being *with* one another, but rather being alone next to one another – let's say sitting on the sofa while each scrolls distractedly through their phone. This is not quality time. It's the worst of both worlds, in that you will quickly get tired of one another's presence, all the while never really being close. Katie and I make sure to spend a few nights every week doing our own thing. When we're together, we make sure that it's deliberate and that we focus on one another.

Create temporal distance

That is, distance in time. Find a little breathing room by remembering that you don't have to share the exact same schedules or be working on the same timelines. As I already mentioned, Katie and I have our own daily and weekly rhythms, and we are often out of one another's orbits when we pursue our own hobbies, work and interests. We allow ourselves time to miss one another.

Bring in the unexpected

I know it can be difficult to be spontaneous, but the more rigidly scheduled your life, the more you could probably benefit from something out of the blue once in a while. One day I secretly arranged a babysitter for the kids and told Katie that morning, "pack an overnight bag and be ready to leave this evening at 6. I'm taking you out somewhere for a surprise." Katie was like a kid at Christmas dying to guess what I had planned for us. We snuck out for a romantic evening just for us. Sure, I had a lot of organizing to do, but for Katie it was fun and unexpected and exciting. We were so buzzed the waiter at the restaurant thought it was our first date.

Reconnect with yourselves as individuals

I once got the opportunity to watch Katie give a lecture to an auditorium of more than 50 students. I got to see a side of her I'd never seen before… and it was surprisingly attractive. She looked so competent, so comfortable in her own world, a world that had nothing to do with me. I was reminded all at once what an absolute catch she was.

Can you find ways to see your partner in a new light like this? Forget about all the old, well-worn topics of conversation, and remind yourself that you don't know everything about them, and that they have a life beyond the one you share with them. I know that Katie and I have the best conversations when we've both gone off and had our separate adventures. When we reconnect, we have so much fresh material to share with one another.

Week 8 Exercise

This week, your task is to find ways to bring in a little distance to your relationship – the juicy, magnetic kind of distance. Now, this can't be a paint-by-numbers thing, so you'll have to brainstorm some ideas that will work for you and your partner. Nevertheless, here are a few ideas for scheduling a "date night" this week where you can start playing with creating that exciting energy in the gap between you.

- Do something completely new. Forget about all your routine food spots, favorite TV shows or everyday routines. Eat somewhere different, explore a new spot in your neighborhood or try cooking a new recipe together. Nothing romantic ever happened in your rut.

- Separately go on your own mini adventures and come back and share your experience with your partner. I know this sounds counterintuitive, but believe me, it works.

- Play a game. Adult life can get serious and boring. Instead, why not play some nostalgic games from your childhood – the sillier the better. A little friendly competition often leads to flirtation.

- Get primal. Go camping in the remote wilderness or do a very physical activity that will reconnect you both to your bodies. That could be dancing, a gourmet meal, wild swimming, or even a spa day where you can both luxuriate together away from the stress and drama of daily life.

- Look through old photos together or reminisce about how you first met. We all take for granted how we felt in the early days – but your partner is still that same awesome person they were then!

- Do a DIY project together, go to the museum or a comedy night, try rock-climbing or stargazing or a concert or a dinner cruise or just building a pillow fort in your living room. Whatever it is, imagine you've only known your partner for a week and are still trying to impress them.

Keely and Mike

Keely and Mike were both into drama at school and are very creative types. They agree to meet up every month at a certain time and place, only they both pretend to be completely different people – right down to dressing up and changing their names, accents, everything. They never break character.

They meet one another at a bar or restaurant and the play acting begins, their respective characters having never met before. They assure me this role play game has little to do with sex. Rather, it's something that they enjoy doing together, but without it ever becoming rote and predictable. Each of them relishes these evenings, precisely because nobody ever knows exactly how things will play out. The morning after, they meet as themselves at the breakfast table and say, "you'll never guess the fascinating person I met last night..."

Week 9

Overcoming Challenges

"It is not our purpose to become each other; it is to recognize each other, to learn to see the other and honour him for what he is."

~ Hermann Hesse

No EFT for couples' book would be complete without a few words on conflict resolution. Whole libraries could be written (have been written) on this topic, but the way I see it, conflict resolution is not all that complicated. It's the easiest thing in the world to fall into conflict, but it takes some presence of mind, compassion and skill to disentangle yourself from a conflict that's already underway.

In EFT, conflict is normal and expected. It's human. However, there are more and less effective ways of dealing with it when it arises. I'll begin by sharing with you the insight that helped me personally begin to develop these skills, and it's this: conflict is not about facts, but feelings. I resisted this realization for a long time; I saw the world as largely a zero-sum game, and conflict as a natural and inevitable outcome of people vying for limited resources. I saw love, respect, understanding and so on as merely one of those resources. That also meant that I believed that if one person "won" then it naturally implied the other person had to "lose."

I now see things very differently.

Let me give you an example to illustrate what I mean about the difference between facts and feelings. You might recognize this kind of story, since it's extremely common. It's common for a reason, however! Our version of the story went like this: Katie came home one day desperately upset. A supervisor at work was more or less bullying her, and she felt under enormous pressure to work around their unfair and unrealistic demands, or risk losing her job.

I listened carefully as she explained the situation, tearful, and how she had no idea what to do. By now, we had had plenty of active listening practice together, and I was doing a pretty good job reflecting, summarizing and empathizing with the core emotion she was expressing: frustration. Then all of a sudden, I wasn't doing so well.

"He's trying to get me fired!" Katie sobbed.

"Come on, that's probably not true. He just sounds like a jerk, but I'm sure he doesn't want to get you fired" I replied.

"He does. He hates me. I don't know why but he just has it in for me!"

"But is that really true? Come on, you can't know that for sure. What exactly did he say? Is he this way with the others? What do your colleagues of him?"

And that right there is where I went wrong. I was looking at what was clearly an emotional situation (my wife's frustration, fear and anger at being unfairly targeted) and treating it like a fact-finding mission. The truth is, it didn't matter one bit what the supervisor did or didn't say, or how he said it, or whether other people concurred with my wife in her perception of him, and so on. No matter what those were, the fact remained: she felt the way she felt.

I was getting distracted by useless detail when I should have been paying attention to what was right in front of me – she was upset and needed consolation. What she did *not* need was for me to come in and tell her the facts, or decide whether I found her reaction rational or not. She did not need the invalidation that came with me actively looking for a second opinion before I considered hers a legitimate one. You won't be surprised that within in a few short minutes, she angrily blurted, "why the hell are you taking his side on this?" I felt stung, but on second thoughts, she was right. I wasn't on her side.

I tell you this little tale to emphasize the fact that when it comes to conflict or strong negative emotions, we usually tend to focus on all the wrong things. If we focus on emotions, however, we give ourselves the best chance of rapidly dissolving those negative feelings – whether we're the ones to "blame" for them or not. If I had seen what Katie was communicating *emotionally* ("I'm hurt and angry and upset! Please comfort me and tell me you can see how upset I am! Please tell me I'm not alone in this. Please care about me") then I could have responded to her *emotionally* ("Wow, what a jerk! What happened next? Come here and tell me all about it. I'm sorry you've had such a hard day, it sounds difficult…").

Sometimes, we can be too literal. Yes, human beings need to actively solve problems in their lives and look for practical solutions. But in conflicts, the problem is usually a lack of emotional connection. It may look on the surface like an argument about unwashed dishes or a missed anniversary, but it's never about these details – it's about the emotion underneath them.

Similarly, when a couple are in conflict with one another, the way out of that conflict is not to dwell on the facts or details, or what one or both may call the "truth." Let me outline for you what happened next with the argument between Katie and me.

She accused me of "taking his side."

I was offended at this. I was only trying to help! I acted like she was being irrational. She couldn't put her finger on what this guy had done, right?

She saw this as a clear attack on her. She defended herself by carefully listing all the things he'd done.

I questioned her about one of these ways, pointing out that that she had probably misunderstood the situation.

She threw her hands in the air and walked off, angry.

By now you should be able to recognize why this argument happened the way it did. It was as though the real emotional conversation was happening underneath, hidden, while a second, completely arbitrary conversation was flowing over the top of it. If our emotions could have talked, they would have said something like this:

I feel so attacked and upset right now. I feel so alone and unsure of myself. Can you reassure me?

Of course. I'm here for you, and you're not alone. I'm sorry you're upset.

No mention of the supervisor, or what the supervisor did or said, or who is right, or who is wrong. It's not about any of that. Many people would recoil from such a blatantly emotional way of speaking because it seems like the problem goes unsolved. The irony is that if I had just said the above words to my wife, she would have calmed down far quicker, and *then* we could have had a genuinely productive conversation about how she was going to handle things. If I had insisted on dwelling on useless details, however, her upset would only have lingered and soon we ourselves would be in a major conflict with one another.

An even trickier challenge is when the reason your partner is unhappy is *you*. It's so easy to jump to defensiveness, clinging to facts and details and the "truth" to try and prove your innocence, all the while missing the *emotional fact* – your partner is hurt.

Resolving conflicts is never easy, no matter how good at communication you are. But here are a few pointers that just might make the difference:

1. Listen for the emotional content of what is being shared with you, rather than focusing on the facts and details.

2. Listen for unmet needs and consider what your partner is ultimately asking you for in this conflict.

3. In the same way, use feeling-talk to express what *you're* really upset about, and ask as clearly as you can for what you need.

4. If you need to, take some space and time to yourself. Step away, catch your breath and return to the conversation when you're feeling calmer and less threatened. There's no rush.

5. Stick to one issue at a time – bringing up old grievances only muddies the water and puts them on the defensive.

6. Avoid blaming and insults, and don't play the victim, even if you genuinely think you are.

7. Finally, a big one: assume that your partner has good intentions. Assume that they don't want to hurt you (remember the work we did on trust?). Most arguments are overblown misunderstandings. Do not take it as an automatic given that your partner *means* to cause you upset. Communicate to them loud and clear that you have good intentions, too. Just because you're in an argument, it doesn't mean that you don't love and care for one another.

Week 9 Exercise

We'll look at two exercises to work on this week; one that you can practice anytime to finetune your communication and empathy skills, and the other to pull out in an emergency, i.e. when an argument is already underway.

Exercise 1

This is a role play exercise that will broaden your ability to acknowledge and respect your partner's perspective. If we get trapped in our own perspective, we can start to perceive our partner as an aggressor or villain, and this makes it impossible to reach a compromise or understanding. For this exercise, each of you will be role-playing the other. You play them, they play you.

Of course, this takes some effort – obviously do not be insulting or superficial about it, but really try to inhabit your partner's world view. For five or ten minutes, have a conversation about something mundane but through the eyes of your partner, from within what you understand to be their worldview. Furthermore, respond to yourself as though you were them.

When you're done, stop the exercise and share your experience with your partner. What did you both get right? What was absolutely wrong? Why was it wrong? What misunderstandings and assumptions does this highlight for you? It can sometimes be very surprising to see how our partner experiences us, not to mention how they assume we think and feel. This exercise can be a goldmine for uncovering blind spots.

Exercise 2

In the midst of a full-blown disagreement, however, the trick is to slow things right down, take a breath and try to simplify. Think of how you might approach a sudden knotty tangle you find in a length of rope – don't pull, don't lose your temper. Just look carefully and try to pull the pieces apart slowly and intelligently.

Here's a simple format to draw on so that you can be sure you're expressing your perspective and your needs while staying receptive to your partner's:

1. Acknowledge the disagreement and set a collaborative tone. Express your sincere desire to resolve it.

2. Clearly lay out your perspective and your feelings.

3. Clearly lay out your needs and what you would like to happen next.

4. Ask for them to share their perspective, feelings and needs and listen actively as they tell you.

Note the order: first, "come in peace." Once you've expressed yourself, invite them to express themselves. For example: "OK, so I see we're clearly not on the same page with this. Can we talk this through? The way I see it, there's no way we can afford to go on that trip, so when you say you insist on going, I feel really anxious and confused. I'd really love for us just to stay home this summer, like we agreed. Can you tell me more about what you're thinking here? I really want to understand."

From there the disagreement can go in any direction, but chances ae if it begins this way, it will eventually resolve amicably. Try other phrases like:

"Let's work through this together."

"What do you need right now?"

"I can see how I've contributed to this problem."

"I really understand what you're saying. I have a different take on things."

"So, you're saying [...], have I understood?"

"When you said/did [...] I felt [...]."

Kit and Maya

Both Kit and Maya have exes who gave them the "silent treatment." As a result, they're both determined that whenever there's a problem, they stop immediately and do what it takes to resolve that tension, rather than letting it build up. The two have developed their own special language specifically for managing conflict. Their in-joke is to call these tension-defusing discussions, "state of the nation addresses" after some long-running joke. The rule is that if either feels like something is amiss, they can instantly "call for a state of the nation address." They do not let things rest until they both feel heard and have reconnected through whatever conflict was emerging.

Week 10

The Art of Relationship Maintenance

"Happily ever after is not a fairy tale, it's a choice." ~ Fawn Weaver

Imagine, if you will, a couple walking together in the wilderness. They walk side-by-side, hand-in-hand. They're walking *together*, and they're heading in roughly the same direction. Occasionally, one of them gets a little distracted by something off to the side. They veer towards it, and the other notices the tug on their hand as the space between them grows wider. Feeling this connection, the first partner recognizes they've strayed and returns, so that they are soon walking comfortably in tandem again.

Occasionally, one of them will have to stop and crouch down to tie a shoelace that's come undone, or brush some thorns or seed heads from their pants. The other one can instantly notice that this has happened (because they're holding hands throughout) and so they can easily stop and wait patiently for the first partner to resolve the issue. Then, they are easily able to walk in tandem again.

Imagine, now, a different couple, walking together in the same wilderness. This couple, however, is not holding hands at all; in fact, they're walking any which way they like, and for a time they're headed in the same direction. However, when one of them gets distracted by something off to the side, the other doesn't notice this distraction, and they keep walking. The distance between them widens, often without them realizing it. Sometimes, one stops to tie their shoelace, and when they stand up again, see that the other one has continued walking, and is now far ahead – perhaps even out of sight.

If such a couple continue to talk in this way, and almost never check in with one another, they might well find after a few hours that there is a mile of distance between them, and they are quite lost to each other. It may take a while for them to realize just how far apart they've strayed, and when they do, it will take a lot of effort to bring them back together again.

I hope you can see the point I'm making with this analogy: when travelling together as a couple, making many frequent, tiny course corrections is something you can do easily and with hardly any effort. Doing so saves you from having to completely backtrack once the problem has grown too far out of hand. The first couple is constantly making these little course corrections, and as a result those corrections stay little. The second couple only need to solve one problem – but by the time they get to solving it, how big that problem is!

This is the idea I want to explore in this chapter, and the secret behind what I call relationship maintenance. To put it very briefly: deal with your small problems before they become big problems. In the previous module, I covered some ways that you might defuse and resolve outright arguments and conflicts. The trick, of course, is to deal with things in such a way as to seldom have those big conflicts in the first place.

Notice how the first couple stay on top of the little niggles: they hold hands. They maintain a connection. The distractions and untied shoelaces in a couple's everyday life are *constant*. Let's call these things "stress." Everyday chores, bills, work, groceries, commuting, walking the dog, fixing dinner, dealing with surprise guests, getting bad news, filling the car with gas, returning that package, filing taxes, buying toothpaste, resolving the fight between your two-year-old and your five-year-old…

All of these things have the potential to knock your relationship off track, just a teeny tiny bit – if you let them, that is. Without realizing it, you may gradually lose connection with your partner. You no longer notice what mood they're in, or when they're having a hard time. You're no longer on the same wavelength. Sometimes, you're both so stressed it feels like you're not even on the same planet. You're like the couple who looks up after an hour and realizes you're both now miles apart.

Relationship maintenance sounds like just one more boring chore to do, but it isn't – relationship maintenance is the small stuff you do *so that you don't have to do the big stuff.* It makes life simpler, not harder. When you're the first couple, the fact that you're holding hands means you never really get the chance to drift too far apart before bouncing back together again. After many years of marriage to my wife, I now feel so well attuned to her that I can just look at her face and instantly tell the mood she's in, and what she most needs from me that day. The trick to this superpower, of course, is that I have to consistently look into her face in the first place! I can't do that if I'm too distracted with my own stress and problems.

Have you ever met a couple where the woman leaves after years and the man is left bewildered, claiming she did it "out of the blue"? I can promise you that there was nothing out of the blue about it. That man lost his wife one small step at a time… but he only noticed the final step.

Most of us realize the importance of having daily stress management techniques so that we are regularly discharging any pent-up tension. But the same is true of relationships; if relational stressors are not regularly addressed and released, they can build up in exactly the same way. The biggest mistake I see couples making in this area is the one I made myself: I thought, "if it ain't broke don't fix it" and assumed that if Katie was unhappy about something, she'd say so sooner or later. But why wait? It's a little like having a houseplant and only watering once the leaves are drooping and going yellow. The time to water was long, long before that point.

Daily stress management rituals

The first thing to realize is that life is stressful – for you, for your partner, for everyone. Because it's inevitable, it just makes sense to actively manage daily stressors as they arise. Some couples do this naturally, but others (especially those who have a more avoidant attachment style) may turn a blind eye to small troubles brewing.

Whereas ordinary stress management is just about you as an individual, relationship stress management is about being aware of how daily troubles and worries are impacting you as a couple – then, obviously, taking steps to address those as soon as possible. These rituals could take on many forms, but it's up to you as a team to decide what it would look like for you. Each of us has a different tolerance level for how much "checking in" we need or are comfortable with, but the most important thing is to maintain consistency. Here are some of the ways couples have developed their own rituals for supporting one another through the daily stress of life.

Jeanie and Ben like to catch up with one another over dinner. They both lead stressful lives and feel like their workdays are spent putting out fires. Their agreement, however, is that once dinner is ready and on the table, couple time begins. This is the special part of the day they reserve for them and them alone. They check in with each other, and genuinely listen. They enjoy their food and enjoy one another's company – with all phones and devices on mute in the next room.

To begin with, they just relax. It takes a few minutes to let off the steam of the day and get into a different state of mind. It's only after the meal, when they might get started on a warm cup of tea or a little dessert, when they allow themselves to broach any unresolved issues. This gives everyone time to connect first, to find one another, and to ease into things. They can't do this every day, of course; sometimes they have to reach out to one another at the McDonalds drive through, and other times they need to catch up over breakfast. But they seldom skip this part of the day. Ninety nine percent of the time there is no big issue to broach at all; but when there is something, the two already have the time and space carved out to tackle it at once.

Chris and Jennifer do things differently. They have their routine Saturday morning brunch together every week if they can, and they use this time to de-stress, forget about life for a while and just remind themselves how much they like to sip on lattes and talk for hours. If a special day is near, they might buy a present for one another or do a little something extra afterwards. The key is that during this time, they're not doing anything else but taking care of *them*. There is no multitasking, no worry about the coming week. Just them.

Doesn't seem like much, does it? But really good couple maintenance is like that – you know you're doing it right because of how easy it feels. I want to finish by telling you about a close friend of mine who took a long time to understand the value of this kind of regular relationship top-up. He would often complain that his girlfriend was constantly nagging him to "have a talk" and he'd dread it, knowing he was in for hours of long, drawn out conversation that was usually emotionally overwrought and exhausting for him.

Trust me, his position was one I understood well. But I had to explain to him that he might have been making problems for himself. His girlfriend, just like Katie, had an insecure and anxious attachment style. According to him, the only problem in their relationship was her relentless need to talk and talk and talk. He couldn't understand her desire to regularly touch base and be reassured. So, he'd avoid things until she'd get so upset that she'd announce that another big talk was in order.

Today, things are a little different with them both. He's now caught on to the idea that the best way to avoid these genuinely grueling conversations is to *keep connected* to his girlfriend. He noticed that when he made the effort to regularly check in and ask how she was feeling and how her day was, she seemed much calmer and happier. When he followed up on little things she'd shared with him the day before, or took extra care to wish her a good night, she seemed less clingy and demanding. No longer was he summoned for the big serious chats.

He soon learnt that all those times his upset girlfriend told him, "We need to talk" what she was really saying was, "We haven't been connecting enough, and that scares me." To return to our couple-in-the-wilderness analogy, my friend realized that if he reached out and grasped his girlfriend's hand, and kept an eye out on her, she never got lost and upset. The irony is that my friend, in wanting to maintain his independence and an easy life, was regularly getting so lost that his partner was freaking out and calling the mountain rescue helicopter, so to speak!

During your check up, you don't need to formally sit down for a big ol' therapy session. Instead, just take an "emotional reading" of where your partner is, and take the chance to fill them in on what you're currently experiencing.

- How are they feeling?

- What do they most feel they need right now?

- Is there anything they'd love to share with you? Something they're excited/grateful/confused about? Something they're finding interesting?

- Are there any upcoming stresses and demands, and how might you both prepare for them?

- Is there anything unsaid that you wish to share? Something you could have done better, or perhaps something someone wants to get off their chest?

- Is there something positive to celebrate? Something nice you'd like to do for one another?

Week 10 Exercise

You guessed it, this week you and your partner are invited to devise a stress management ritual of your own. Whether your stress is related to work, childcare, money worries, daily housework, family, or just navigating the craziness of the world, you need to decide together how you're going to carve out a little sanctuary just for you both.

This does *not* have to be complicated or cost any money. What it does have to be is regular, so make sure you're both choosing something you can comfortably commit to. Decide on:

- How often you want to check in

- How long you want to check in for

- When you want to check in

- What you want to do during these periods

- How you'll adjust if things change, or you can't complete the ritual

During the twelve-week program you may find yourself talking a lot more than you ordinarily would, but the schedule you decide on today will be something that continues long after the program is finished.

Leah and Julian

"We have loads of little rituals. My favorite is our bedtime routine. We chill out in bed with the dog and listen to an audiobook together, then we chat afterwards and then go to sleep. Sometimes the chat is short, sometimes we end up talking about the deep and meaningfuls late into the night… but it's something we end every day with. It's like coming home."

Week 11

Pause for Reflection

"Love does not begin and end the way we seem to think it does. Love is a battle, love is a war; love is a growing up." ~ James Baldwin

At this point, it will have been just over two months since you embarked on the program and set out some mutual relationship goals. A lot can change in two months – what's changed for you?

We have two more modules remaining, and that means it's a great time to stop, gather up our thoughts, and see how far we've come. We began our journey with an appraisal of our respective attachment styles, and how they may influence the way we communicate, solve problems and seek to have our needs met.

I remember wondering once whether it was possible to change one's attachment style. Was I doomed to be avoidant all my life? Would I always be that little bit more reluctant, detached and mistrustful of others just because of experiences that happened decades ago?

Opinions on this differ, but I strongly believe that if it *is* possible to change one's attachment style, then the way it would be altered is the same way it was introduced in the first place: through relationships. Consider that for many of us, a big part of our initial attraction to our partners was our own unresolved attachment trauma. For example, we attached insecurely, and ended up repeating that same dynamic we learnt from our early relationship models with every adult relationship ever after.

This means that we may be attracted to precisely those people most suited to replaying our unhealthy patterns. Is this a good thing or a bad thing? I believe the answer to that comes down to the level of conscious awareness you have, and how well you master the kind of work we've covered in this book so far.

If your attachment traumas drive you repeatedly into the arms of people whose own attachment traumas mean they're really good at pushing your "buttons" then you are presented with an opportunity. Well, two opportunities. The first is that you get the choice to play out the pattern all over again, in just the same way as you have before. The second opportunity is that you get that chance to finally work *through* this dynamic, to resolve it, to heal it, and to come out the other side. Your partner, then, could be either your nemesis or your greatest teacher. What they become to you depends not on them, but on you.

The best long-term relationships are those where each half has mutually found a way to intensify but also heal the worst tendencies in the other. Katie sometimes drove me mad; she'd challenge me to face exactly those things I'd spent my life avoiding; she pushed me to own my own woundedness and vulnerability; she repeatedly invited me to address the little pain in my heart that made it terrifying to reach out to others, to risk needing them, and to have blind, tender faith in their ability to respond to me.

The lessons went the other way, too. All of my worst attributes – my stubborn independence, my inability to commit, my selfishness – all of these things were like a powerful medicine that taught Katie that she was stronger than she knew, more complete, more whole as the fascinating and beautiful woman she was. I taught Katie a lesson she could not have learnt from someone more psychologically healthy: that sometimes, you need to reach that breaking point where you fully let someone go, with your blessing, knowing that you are and always have been enough for yourself.

I can sometimes wax poetic on this topic, but I sincerely think that if couples can summon enough patience, bravery and kindness, they can discover in one another exactly what they need to put the wounds of the past to rest.

Culturally, we have this fairytale idea of "The One" and how perfect it would be to love them forever. I think the reality is a little different; we find our soul mates in the flawed people all around us, here and now. We don't discover one another, perfectly formed and individuated, healthy and strong. We find one another in pieces, halfway through a process, patched together, and imperfect. But then, if we do things right, we can find our way to health and wholeness *together.*

I also want to share a quick caveat on something that relationship books sometimes gloss over: the question of when and how to end a relationship. I don't want you to think of a breakup as a failure, or an ongoing relationship as a success. Rather, I want to encourage you to think of another metric entirely. Have you treated this other person, this soul, this human being, with respect, consideration and kindness? Have you been all that you can be with them, i.e. honest? Have you spoken from your heart, and have you listened from the same place?

If you have done all this, then your relationship is a "success", whether it lasts a month or thirty years. Without these things, a relationship is nothing more than a mindless habit, something running on momentum, a script read by the assigned actors in the play.

This week, I invite you as a couple to pause and dwell on how your own attachment tendencies have changed over time, and how they are impacting your connection to your partner. Through the exercises in this book, you are not only developing joint emotional intelligence, but also subtly changing the old patterns you learnt long ago. We keep these patterns alive through our behavior now, in the present. Every time we connect and interact with our partner, we have an opportunity to behave differently, and to start setting down different patterns and habits.

Where we have mistrusted others, we can choose to let go and have faith in the good intentions of others.

Where we have felt alone, unworthy and unloved, we can choose to love ourselves, to ask boldly for what we need, and to seek belonging.

Where we have felt lack and insecurity (and our own selfishness), we can choose to lavish love on others, to sacrifice, to experience the joy of giving.

Where we have felt confused and misunderstood, we can choose to reach out, to communicate our thoughts and feelings, and to stand tall in our own authenticity.

Let's take another look at the characteristics of a securely attached adult, as we covered back in the first week of the program. We saw that securely attached adults are:

- Comfortable and confident in who they are as people

- Not afraid that others will abandon, reject or dislike them

- Able to give and receive love easily

- Good communicators, who are at ease expressing their needs and limits

- Able to be intimate but enjoy independence too

With the previous ten weeks in mind, which of the above characteristics are you feeling more confident in? Which still need your focus and, more importantly, how might you use your relationship as a platform on which to learn these new skills and abilities? Don't be surprised to see that your partner is developing skills that are the mirror opposite of the ones you're developing.

Your insights

I often think that people already know full well what's best for them, they only need enough experts to say the same thing for long enough before they feel they have permission to know what they already know! This week, I want you to check in with yourself and ask about all those things that you know, but might not know you know.

To guide the uncovering of these insights, try journalling with the following prompts. You can write any or all of the following sentence stems at the top of the page and then, without thinking too much about it, complete the sentence as you see fit. Some of these may resonate more than others.

When I was younger, I learnt that other people are _____ *and that I am* _____ .

What I most need from other people is _____ .

What I most have to offer other people is _____ .

I have had a difficult time receiving _____.

I have a difficult time giving _____.

I chose my current partner because _____.

I believe my current partner chose me because _____.

My partner is teaching me _____.

I am teaching my partner _____.

Since the start of the course, _____ has changed.

If there was one thing I wanted my partner to know, it would be that _____.

I most need to forgive _____.

I am sorry for _____.

My gift is _____.

I need help with _____.

This course would have been perfect if only it included _____.

The best thing I'm taking from this course is _____.

If I could say just one thing to my younger self, it would be _____.

If I could say just one thing to my partner when they were a child, it would be _____.

As you work through these journal prompts, you may uncover insights and ideas you wish to share with your partner, or you may simply mull over them privately. The thing about being in a relationship, however, is that your growth is the relationship's growth. The more self-awareness, compassion and insight you develop within yourself, the more you can bring to the table, and the more your partner will benefit. Th connection between you cannot help but strengthen.

This is perhaps why some psychologists think that the best way to correct an insecure attachment bond is to build a relationship with a person who is securely attached. In time, simply by being who they are, such securely attached individuals can teach the rest of us to be calmer, more loving, and more trusting. In the same way, you can expand the boundaries of your own concept of "personal development" and realize that as you work out your own issues, you are making yourself the best possible partner for the person you love. This, in turn, helps them grow and be the best partner for *you* that they can be.

Week 11 Exercise

This week, sit down with your partner and devise an updated plan for your relationship going forward. I'm leaving this exercise deliberately open-ended because nobody knows your relationship better than you do. Making use of the skills developed so far, discuss:

1. Your short-, medium- and long-term goals for the relationship

2. Your personal goals, and how they fit into the relationship

3. Any new boundaries and limits you want to renegotiate

4. Any unresolved questions, issues or problems you want to continue working on

In the final module next week, we'll be ending our journey together in the best way I know how: celebrating! We'll take time to appreciate both individual and shared achievements, and recommit to a renewed relationship together with a ritual to recognize all our hard work and patience.

This week, however, is about taking stock. There may be some negativity or unwelcome emotions, and there may be a completely amazing sense of fresh gratitude for your partner. There may be a realization of much hard work is needed to move on, and there may be a feeling of relief and trust in your renewed connection. There may be a mix of all these things! Your job this week is to simply weigh up where you are and what you've gained from the process. It's also to check in with your partner and compare notes.

Vicky and Leo

By the time this couple reached the end of the program, their relationship was unrecognizable. Both had done significant work rethinking their old assumptions, limits and fears, and they had done this work together, too, contemplating from scratch what they really wanted from themselves, from life, from one another. After a bumpy ride, the two came out with a new appreciation of how they would need to learn to manage life's transitions together as a couple if they hoped to stick together. They consider themselves more in sync now, and have been learning as they go. Vicky shared how none of her prior relationships had lasted longer than a year, but her and Leo have now been married for six years. "I like to tell people that I have ended my marriage and started again a hundred times over... I just always do it with the same man."

Week 12

Celebrate!

"True love stories never have endings." ~ Richard Bach

If you've made it this far, well done.

We're just about ready to take those training wheels off and ride off into the sunset, so to speak. I know that relationship work can get heavy sometimes, and making genuine changes demands a lot of us. That said, the final week of the program is the time to acknowledge and celebrate where you are, and pause to relish just how much there is to be thankful for.

I want to share one final anecdote, and this one I'll call the Tale of the Automatic Chocolate. Katie has always experienced quite disruptive PMS symptoms, and spends a few days every month basically possessed with the desire to eat vast quantities of chocolate (I know, I know – my wife is straight out of a cheesy sitcom). I soon realized that I could easily lighten her burden and do something practical to help by supplying said chocolate. One day, it dawned on me that I was not consistently doing this every month; rather, I was constantly having to remind myself to drop by the store on the way home and pick her up some of her favorite chocolates. Sometimes it just slipped my mind.

I decided there and then to arrange for an automated delivery of chocolate once a month – every month – so that I would never forget. Yes, it's a pretty small thing in the grand scheme. But I no longer take small things for granted. By basically subscribing to this small kindness once a month, I made kindness to my wife automatic – in other words, I made it so it was impossible for me not to show her kindness.

This week, as you celebrate all the wonderful things you've either created anew or rediscovered, I also encourage you to think about how you might bank these gains, and make them as automatic as a monthly chocolate delivery. What we make a habit no longer requires any conscious effort. That's a good place to be; you want your default status with your partner to always be positive, so that it would actually take effort to shift out of this healthy pattern.

In this way, you can future-proof your relationship against all those bumps and snags that you'll inevitably find in the road ahead. My simple gesture means that I never get to a state where I am unresponsive to my wife's monthly discomfort. No matter what's happening in the world, or how close or distant we may be, she can always assume that there is another instalment of chocolate coming, because I care about her.

You get it – the chocolate is just a symbol here. Your relationship habits don't have to be material. Rather, you can commit to your daily stress management routines as a couple, regularly check in with one another emotionally, make frequent "deposits" into the trust account, and schedule time that is reserved for you as a couple to simply have fun and do something a little unexpected. The more automatic you make this, the more robust a partnership you build.

This week, can you think of any gains you've made either individually or as a couple, that you'd like to cement in? As you celebrate and give thanks for this achievement, can you also think of ways to cultivate it in the long term, so that it keeps growing?

When Katie and I completed our own EFT couples' course, we felt like we'd definitely earnt a treat. The kids were packed off to their grandparents and we booked a small getaway for just the two of us for a couple days. It was expensive and difficult to organize, but it was more than worth it. With this little trip, we were both saying to one another, "This matters. *We* matter. Our relationship is worth investing in." We decided we wanted to create our very own relationship renewal ritual. We spoke about it at length on the journey over, and got excited about all the little details. It felt on the one hand like a silly kids' game, and on the other it was as serious as renewing wedding vows.

I won't tell you in detail how we renewed this sense of love and commitment to one another – I'm sure the only two people in the world our ritual will make sense to are the two people who were there that day! But I also know that you'll have your own ideas about what would feel most emotionally satisfying for you and your partner. How can you celebrate this milestone and enjoy one another? How can you symbolically and ritualistically let go of everything that needs to be let go, while embracing all the wonderful new things you've just begun?

One thing I will say is that the day we came home from our trip, we kept saying to one another, "we should do this more often!" Why had we never thought to take time just to *enjoy* ourselves, and one another? We had just bumbled along for years, demanding so much from our connection and only bothering to tend to it when it started to give us problems. Instead, why not deliberately honor just how awesome your partner is, and just how lucky you are to get to love them, by having a celebration all to yourselves?

I'm not just talking about going on some pricy couples' spa package or splashing out on a meal or a hotel. I'm talking about unapologetically indulging in things you both love... and having fun! Half the fun can be deciding exactly what that means. Sit down together and make a couples' "bucket list" – be creative and daring – or take a trip down memory lane and revisit some old hobbies or activities that you haven't paid much attention to lately. Do things simply for the reason that they give you pleasure to do them, and if you both deserve a pat on the back for doing the best you can for one another, now's the time for that too.

A note on disappointment

It wouldn't be fair to end this program without addressing the more difficult aspects, i.e. all those regrets, hurts, disappointments, losses and difficult feelings that might still remain. I get it. Twelve weeks is a long time, but in some ways it's also just the blink of an eye. Try not to hold yourself or your partner to unreasonable expectations about where you "should" be at this point. Just because the program has ended, it doesn't mean that you "should" live happily ever after, with all your issues and worries put to bed forever more.

This can be a delicate time, but be kind. Be patient. Return now to your original goals set in the second week and see how you fared. We set those goals to help us stay mindful and focused on what matters to us – not to punish ourselves with arbitrary pressures and demands. You may have discovered that your goal needed a lot of tweaking. Or you may have easily reached your goal and then discovered that you actually want to set a new, completely different one. You may have come through the twelve-week journey only to discover that the goal you set is really part of a bigger issue, one that now requires some action or choice that you hadn't considered in the beginning. All of this is OK. All of these are legitimate outcomes.

Recall our four EFT principles that we looked at right in the beginning of the book:

Emotions are dynamic and experiential: The work unfolds in the here and now, in the connection, in the conversation. A relationship is a living, breathing thing that always changes.

Emotions require our awareness: You cannot understand your emotions or those of others unless you can acknowledge and accept them first.

Emotions need to be expressed: To reach out and connect with our partners, we need to be able to clearly express our feelings, our needs, and our limitations.

Emotions can be regulated: We are not defined by our emotional experience in any one moment.

Now, your goal may have been to re-kindle a certain kind of relationship with your partner, to overcome certain difficulties or, yes, live happily ever after. I want to invite you, however, to use a different yardstick for measuring whether you have made progress. Guided by the above principles, ask yourself the following questions:

Have you improved your ability to stay more conscious and connected in the moment?

Have you remained open-minded and curious about the possibility of change in yourself and in your relationship?

Have you learnt more about yourself, your feelings, your needs, wants and weaknesses? Are you more self-aware?

Have you expressed yourself with honesty and respect? Have you honored your experience and those of your partner?

Finally, have you made efforts to improve on your weaknesses, as well as forgive and accept the weaknesses of others?

I'll be honest with you, some people walking through the couples' therapy door do not come out again as a couple. They may realize that there are certain fundamental incompatibilities, or that it would be healthier and wiser for both to move on. But if they have learnt how to understand themselves a little more, how to communicate, how to ask for what they need, how to forgive themselves and others for being human, how to regulate stress and how to trust and connect, then they have not failed. I truly believe that a couple that breaks up with this much compassion and consciousness is a more successful couple than one that persists but only because of avoidance, coercion, ignorance or fear.

Week 12 Exercise

Time to decide how you and your partner want to close off this twelve-week journey. Every single couple will be different, and they'll want to highlight different aspects of the process and make meaning in their own unique ways. One couple may find that romance has blossomed and they want to renew their marriage vows. Or they may decide to take the "next step" together, whether that next step is meeting the parents, moving into together, making a public commitment like marriage, getting a dog, having a baby… or having another baby.

Other couples might decide that what they most need is a little more fun, spontaneity and enjoyment. They may book a celebratory trip or take up a fun new hobby together. For those couples who have already been together for a long time, the best way to mark the end of the program could be to begin something new, turn the page, and start over. This may mean more practical changes to living and working arrangements, or more subtle renewals like a fresh sense of loyalty to one another. For still other couples, the outcome of the process may be new clarity about things that just no longer work, and the courageous acceptance that the best way forward is to separate.

What does it look like for you and your partner?

Zee and Adam

Zee and Adam's relationship had always been difficult. The two were perfect for one another on paper, and both wanted exactly the same things out of life. They were like two of a kind, undeniably soul mates if such a thing existed… but the trouble was they were simply not sexually compatible, and had very little attraction for one another. They worked on their relationship for years, but they were never truly happy. They signed up for an EFT course together, hoping for an answer, and in a way, that's exactly what they got. After completing a twelve-week program similar to the one above, they both felt able at last to address the elephant in the room. Together, with great difficulty, they could mutually admit that a key aspect of their relationship was simply not there.

Did they break up? Yes. They wished with all their hearts they could find a way for it not to matter, but it did. The two spent some time mourning the loss of the future they thought they had with one another, but eventually, something else dawned on them both – they still wanted to be in one another's lives. In the rubble of their old relationship, they discovered something that had been staring them in the face all along: their amazing friendship.

For Zee and Adam, the end was the beginning. In time, both of them moved on and started dating other people, but they remained the closest of friends. In fact, the day after they broke up, they booked a holiday to Switzerland together. They can both laugh about it now. They had avoided talking about the possibility of breaking up for so long, when it was really the relief they had been looking for. Their relationship didn't end at all, it just changed. In fact, it didn't really even change… it just took Zee and Adam a few years to realize what it always had been!

Conclusion

"To say that one waits a lifetime for his soulmate to come around is a paradox. People eventually get sick of waiting, take a chance on someone, and by the art of commitment become soulmates, which takes a lifetime to perfect." ~ Criss Jami

In this book, I've shared many stories with you about the lives of many different couples. In doing so, my hope is that you feel more able to tell your own story – and perhaps start thinking about different ways that story might end. I'd like to conclude with some lessons and insights from the world of emotion-focused therapy, but also some which I've distilled from my own life and the lives of other couples.

Relationships are important... but you should have more than one

For most of human history, people lived in tribes and villages, deeply embedded in their complex social webs and playing many different roles – parent, grandparent, sibling, child, friend. The modern world is more fractured and isolated in comparison, and sadly many of us rely on our partners to substitute for the emotional needs that were once provided by a whole village. Even the healthiest, happiest relationship cannot fulfil our every need, and we won't thrive if we are shouldered with the burden of meeting all our partner's.

Sometimes the best thing we can do for our relationships is give them some space, and pursue rich and meaningful lives outside of them. This means tending to family bonds, building friendships, connecting with the community, perhaps even consulting with a therapist or a spiritual or religious leader. Your partner may well be the most important person in your world, but they cannot *be* your world.

It's not your fault... but you are responsible

There was a young guy in our group who really took to the EFT process and seemed to be getting plenty from it. His girlfriend complained, however, that he was simply using his attachment style as an excuse for poor behavior. It seemed that he had re-examined his own childhood and concluded that a painful lack of connection and care during his formative years had traumatized him. Consequently, he felt no responsibility for his outbursts towards his girlfriend, which were frequent, and came with no apology once he had calmed down. It wasn't his fault, he felt, and couldn't be changed.

You can probably see that this is backward. In EFT, we recognize the historical cause of certain patterns of behavior that we witness in the present. None of us is to blame for the upbringing we received, or the faulty relational habits we learnt in order to cope. Nevertheless, though childhood trauma is not your fault, it is your responsibility – meaning that you are always blessed with the choice, in the present moment, to choose what you do next. The tricky fact is that some of the world's most abusive people were first victims of someone else's abuse; our task is to find acknowledgement and acceptance of this fact, while realizing that someone's trauma never entitles them to perpetuate trauma onto someone else.

In a similar way, causing offense or hurt by accident doesn't mean you are at fault or to blame, but it does mean that you are repsonsible for the consequences. Responsible can be thought of as response-able. It's part of the human experience to feel fear, to have weaknesses, and to make mistakes. It's normal for there to be hurts and misunderstandings. However, it's how you *respond* to these that determines the quality of your relationships.

Your relationship will never be perfect... but it will always have its strengths

Sometimes traveling the path of personal development brings with it an increased awareness of everything that is wrong with us, with our partners and with our relationship. We can get caught in a trap where we notice increasingly small flaws and weaknesses, and get increasingly obsessive about fixing them. It's no exaggeration to say that some people become addicted to self-improvement, and continually seek out its thrills and vindications, long past the point of needing it.

It's worth really understanding that your relationship will never be perfect. If you just think about it for a moment, the entire concept of a "perfect relationship" collapses with just a little consideration for what that would look like, day to day. It's a pure abstraction, and an impossibility. However, if you keep looking for things to fix and improve, don't be surprised when you keep on discovering new things to fix.

Instead, practice gratitude for what is already right. Every relationship, no matter how flawed, has its own beauty and strength and character. It may be a better investment of your energy to focus on these things, rather than nitpick the few details that aren't quite right. Your partner will always possess some annoying, less-than-ideal traits (just like you!). Focus instead on what you love most about them.

Communication is important... but you can communicate too much!

We are an over-therapized culture. Many of us see therapy and self-development as a more or less permanent way of life, and something to infuse into every corner of our being. We may put a lot of emphasis on conscious, verbal communication and dialogue, as though every moment could be a counseling session. But verbal communication of this kind is just one way to connect – and it isn't necessarily the right way, either.

Too much talk can kill spontaneity, introduce confusion and feed into the assumption that there is always something to talk *about*. What's more, emotionally grueling and serious conversations can start to make relationships feel like boring, unrewarding work. During a relationship crisis, it's necessary to talk. But if things are flowing well, try to support your connection in other ways – levity, playfulness and recreation are just as important.

You may have a legitimate complaint... but you won't resolve it until you let it go

Emotion-focused therapists sometimes like to say that we need to switch from a complaints-focus to a solutions-focus. This is easier said than done. We may find ourselves with legitimate gripes and criticisms about things our partner does or has done. We may turn up to the therapy process or to the conversation wanting things to change so badly that we end up harping on that behavior. By this I mean nagging, complaining, or continually bringing up transgressions and expressing our indignation at it all.

I want to tell you: you need to let all this go. Not because you don't have a right to be upset, or because your partner was right to do what they did. Rather, I say this because sometimes the only way to get your needs truly met (and your grievances acknowledged) is paradoxically to set them aside for a moment. When you're focused on complaints, you are not in the headspace to collaborate with your partner to find a solution. Unless you let complaints go (at least temporarily) you won't be able to get down to the work of resolving that conflict and disagreement.

Instead, keep asking yourself, "what can I do right now to reconnect with my partner and help our relationship?" If you're unhappy about something, ask, "how can I communicate my needs to my partner in a way they'll really hear?" If you can do this, and work through the disagreement, you'll find that your grievance disappears naturally on its own. Dwelling on your partner's shortcomings, however, will only emphasize them in your eyes, and put them on the defensive.

Learn from others and get advice… but keep other people out of your relationship

Friends and family almost always mean well and want to help. But in my experience, people who are close to you can be some of the worst to share your relationship trouble with. They may have their own ideas and agendas, and as much as I hate to say it, some people simply relish being around drama and suffering.

We need to be extremely mindful of who we share sensitive details with about our partners and relationships. People cannot be relied on to keep secrets, to stop themselves judging, or to refrain from giving "advice" that is more about them than you. People can be plain old nosy! What's more, sharing personal information about your partner means that you're not taking it up with *them*. This can feel like an incredible breach of trust, and misunderstandings and hurt feelings can abound.

Infidelity is an obvious poison in a relationship, but in my experience the bigger threat comes from weakened boundaries in general. If you're having problems, try seeking help from a counsellor or other neutral third party who can be trusted to respect your confidentiality. Commit to not airing details about your partner to others and make a point of speaking kindly and respectfully about them when they're not present. Likewise, avoid getting involved in other people's gossip about their own partners.

Love is essential… but it's not enough

A modern relationship myth goes like this: when two people are right for each other, they meet and eventually fall in love. Because they're in love, all the other stuff kind of happens as a matter of course. The end.

This story, I probably don't need to tell you, is a recipe for disaster. It's common for people to fall into one another's lives because of love (or just plain chemistry) and then scarcely give a thought to the rest of it. Money, children, housework, what counts as cheating, how often your mother-in-law can visit… these things are tacked on after the fact. But if you could see things from a relationship counsellor's perspective, you'd discover something interesting: few couples complain of not having enough love for their partners. They *do* complain, however, about childcare, and the daily grind, and who pays the bills, and whose job it is to fold the laundry.

If you want to protect your relationship, don't leave all the boring stuff till the last minute. Have proactive conversations about the division of labor in the home, about children, about religion and finances and where you want to live, about family and your obligations to them, about whether you'll get a dog… everything. These things are not an impediment to love and romance. They are the supporting structure that keeps that love and romance safe and flourishing.

Thank You

Thank you so much for purchasing my book.

There were dozens of options, but you took a chance on this book.

Thank you for taking this journey with me and making it all the way to the end.

Before you go, allow me to ask for a tiny favor. Would you please consider posting a review on the platform? It only takes 5 seconds.

Posting a review is the best and easiest way to support the work of independent authors like me.

Your feedback will help me keep writing and sharing the books and resources to propel you towards your desired results.

Hearing from you would mean the world.

https://www.amazon.com/review/create-review

Bibliography

Emotion Focused Therapy

Greenberg, Leslie S.; Johnson, Susan M. (1988). *Emotionally focused therapy for couples.* New York: Guilford Press.

Greenman, P.S. and Johnson, S.M. (2012). Process Research on Emotionally Focused Therapy (EFT) for Couples: Linking Theory to Practice. *Family Process*, 52(1), pp.46–61.

Johnson, Susan M.; Greenberg, Leslie S. (1985a). "Differential effects of experiential and problem-solving interventions in resolving marital conflict". *Journal of Consulting and Clinical Psychology*. **53** (2): 175–184.

Johnson, Susan M.; Greenberg, Leslie S. (1985b). "Emotionally focused couples therapy: an outcome study". *Journal of Marital and Family Therapy*. **11** (3): 313–317.

Johnson, Susan M.; Greenberg, Leslie S. (1987). "Emotionally focused marital therapy: an overview". *Psychotherapy: Theory, Research, Practice, Training*. **24** (3S): 552–560.

Johnson, Susan M.; Greenberg, Leslie S. (1988). "Relating process to outcome in marital therapy". *Journal of Marital and Family Therapy*. **14** (2): 175–183.

Wiebe, Stephanie A.; Johnson, Susan M. (September 2016). "A review of the research in emotionally focused therapy for couples". *Family Process*. **55** (3): 390–407.

Attachment Theory

Abrams, David B.; et al. (2013). "Attachment Theory". *Encyclopedia of Behavioral Medicine*. New York, NY: Springer New York. pp. 149–155.

Johnson, S.M. (2019). *Attachment theory in practice: Emotionally Focused Therapy (EFT) with individuals, couples, and families.* New York, Ny: The Guilford Press.

Johnson, Susan M.; Sims, Ann (2000). "Attachment theory: a map for couples therapy". In Levy, Terry M (ed.). *Handbook of attachment interventions.* San Diego: Academic Press. pp. 169–191.

Simpson J.A. (1999). "Attachment Theory in Modern Evolutionary Perspective". In Cassidy J, Shaver PR (eds.). *Handbook of Attachment: Theory, Research and Clinical Applications.* New York: Guilford Press. pp. 115–40.

Printed in Great Britain
by Amazon

39784095R00078